THE INSIDER'S
52 HOMES IN
52 WEEKS

THE INSIDER'S GUIDE TO
52 HOMES IN
52 WEEKS

Acquire Your
Real Estate Fortune Today

Dolf de Roos, PhD
Gene Burns

WILEY

John Wiley & Sons, Inc.

Published by John Wiley & Sons, Inc., Hoboken, New Jersey.
Published simultaneously in Canada.

For general information on our other products and services please contact our Customer Care Department within the United States at (800) 762-2974, outside the United States at (317) 572-3993 or fax (317) 572-4002.

Wiley also publishes its books in a variety of electronic formats. Some content that appears in print may not be available in electronic books. For more information about Wiley products, visit our web site at www.wiley.com.

Library of Congress Cataloging-in-Publication Data:
De Roos, Dolf.
   The insider's guide to 52 homes in 52 weeks : Acquire Your Real Estate Fortune Today / Dolf de Roos and Gene Burns.
      p. cm.
   ISBN-13: 978-0-471-75705-4 (pbk.)
   ISBN-10: 0-471-75705-5 (pbk.)
   1. Real estate investment.   I. Title.
HD1382.5.D4   2006
332.63'243—dc22   2005023491

Printed in the United States of America.

10 9 8 7 6 5 4 3 2 1

Contents

Introduction   ix

CHAPTER 1   The Real Estate Challenge   1

Who We Are and How the Challenge
    Came About   3
Gene's Early Real Estate Deals   6

CHAPTER 2   What We Did in Vegas and What You Can
Do Anywhere   11

An Explosion of an Experience   13
Why We Chose Las Vegas   15

CHAPTER 3   Determining Your Strategy and
Getting Started   23

Strategy   25
Motivated Sellers   34
Real Estate Acquisition Program (REAP)   42
What It Takes to Succeed   46
Commitment   48
Not All Deals Work   49
Respect for Others   50

CHAPTER 4   Our First Deals   53

Everybody Wins   56
Inspiring Steve   60
The Veteran Who Came Home to Die   63
Four Dobermans and a Private Eye   68
Three Bed, Two Bath, One Trans Am   72

CONTENTS

The Blackjack Dealer's Wife and the
Federal Agent 76

CHAPTER 5   Learning to Ask for Help 81

The Beautiful Girl and the Private Eye 83
Hire a Title Agent 85
Fire and Water 87
Helping a Widower 90
Buyer's Agents 91
When We Party, We Like to Party 95
The "Looks Too Good to Be True,
But It Wasn't" Deal 99
Feeding Frenzy 101
The Big Picture 104

CHAPTER 6   A Shift in Strategies 107

Surrounded by Investors 109
Finding Tenants in Dark Times 110
Mountain and Wall Views 115
A Sun-Room for a Quilter 117
Single Momster 119
Model Lease-Backs 121
Back to Hawaii 123

CHAPTER 7   Networking 127

Gene's Niece 129
Our Lender 129
Our Lender's Loan Officer 130
Tax Lien Homes 130
Our Odds Shift 135
Phase Ones 136
Pretty Views with Bad Golfers 137

CHAPTER 8   Being Flexible 139

Market Changes 141
Success 142

Contents

CHAPTER 9   Why Las Vegas Will Continue to Grow   143

CHAPTER 10   You Can Do It, Too   149

Appendixes   **155**

APPENDIX A   Authorization to Release Information   157

APPENDIX B   Grant, Bargain, and Sale Deed   159

APPENDIX C   Limited Power of Attorney   161

APPENDIX D   Binding Legal Agreement   165

52 Homes—Some Photos   167

Further Tips, Tools, and Information   183

About the Authors   185

Other Books by Dolf de Roos   187

Index   191

Introduction

This book is about two real estate guys who do more than just talk about real estate. They walk the talk—in a huge, adventurous, and daring way. One of them is Dolf de Roos, world-renowned real estate investor, author, and educator. In his first book, which came out some 15 years ago, Dolf said that if you buy one house a year for 10 years, you will be financially free. That was then. This book is not about buying one house a year. It is about a quest to buy one house a week—for an entire year. The other guy is Gene Burns, who started off as Dolf's student, applied his knowledge, worked incredibly hard, and became his partner in a challenge that baffled their friends, tested their resolve and determination, made their real estate agents and mortgage brokers rich, and still has many wondering how they did it.

This book is their story. It is the story of a challenge Dolf set to buy 52 homes in 52 weeks. It is the story of real-life real estate investing under a lot of pressure—pressure to succeed with strict constraints on time and capital used. This is the story of their quest, sometimes messy, sometimes heartbreaking, but always inspiring.

Chapter 1

THE REAL ESTATE CHALLENGE

WHO WE ARE AND HOW THE CHALLENGE CAME ABOUT

Dolf began investing in real estate while studying electrical engineering at the University of Canterbury. By the time he had finished his PhD in the mid-1980s, he had a substantial portfolio. When he had finished his doctorate, he was offered a job paying $32,000 per year, a handsome salary at the time. Unfortunately for his prospective employer, Dolf had just completed a real estate deal that netted him $35,000. The prospect of working an entire year for a lesser amount did not appeal to him. Dolf didn't accept the job, and to this day has never had one. He carried on investing in all manner of real estate. He has invested in everything from homes and apartments to offices, veterinary surgeries, convenience stores, strip malls, funeral parlors, and vineyards. He invests on his own, with partners, and in joint ventures. He is also the founder and chairman of the public company Property Ventures Limited. Apart from being a serious investor, Dolf has always been willing to share what he does and how he does

3

it. Through his books, tapes, videos, software, mentoring programs, weekly video broadcasts, and seminars in more than 16 countries, Dolf has helped tens of thousands of investors achieve financial freedom.

Back in April 2001, Dolf ran a series of seminars for the Learning Annex in California. To convince audiences that it's easy to beat the national average in real estate, he shared the growth rates of the top two U.S. cities in the property market: Las Vegas, Nevada, and Phoenix, Arizona.

Dolf expounded about how significantly higher those cities were than the national average in terms of absolute population growth, proportional population growth, and capital growth of real estate values. He explained, using statistics, graphs, and logic, why these two cities would continue to grow at a higher than average rate for many years to come. Furthermore, unlike many educators on the circuit, Dolf was first and foremost an investor, and taught only as a sideline. He was putting his money where his mouth was. He was not saying, "This is what you should do assuming my theories are correct," but rather "come and do what I'm doing."

In the audience that night, in the front row, sat Gene Burns. A clear real estate novice, he paid attention and responded to questions. From that night on, Gene kept turning up at Dolf's events—evening events, one-day events, weekend events— you name it, Gene was there. He never asked for anything, but he did share, full of enthusiasm, how he had taken the plunge. Dolf inquired which plunge he was referring to, and Gene said, "You know, doing the Vegas thing."

It turned out that after hearing about the state of the real estate market in Las Vegas at that first Learning Annex event, Gene went home and told his wife that they were moving to Vegas to get into real estate.

This represented an enormous change for Gene. Until then he had colored inside the lines of corporate life. He had earned a college degree, started a corporate career immediately after university, and stuck with it. "I got in early and stayed late," he said. He wasn't a political player, but he got along with everybody and was a reliable employee who could be trusted to do a thorough job. He was assigned responsibility for increasingly difficult projects, and became known as the go-to guy in publishing for starting new magazines. When his company had created new publishing concepts, Gene formed a team of salespeople to travel nationally selling the concept and advertising to top accounts. Some of the publications Gene started include *Maximum PC*, *Home PC*, and *Windows Magazine*.

Gene climbed the corporate ladder, made great money, and, in his words, "played by the rules." He took advantage of every 401(k) investment and hired a financial planner, to ensure the financial security of his family and for his retirement. He thought he was doing everything correctly. What he didn't know was that the financial planner and the Human Resources department were as ignorant as he was when it came to investing. Neither ever mentioned the possibility— let alone need—for obtaining some type of investment that would generate passive income. At 46 years of age, he had never even heard the term.

Gene didn't hang with people who invested in real estate. He ran with corporate types who invested in stocks. Rental homes were for losers who had to fix toilets on the weekend while big players like him and his friends played golf and went to resorts. "Why would we ever want to deal with tenants? I was dumb," Gene says now.

Although Gene was a great corporate team player and a specialist in his field, the field was beginning to change. With the birth of online business and the Internet, magazine publishing began to feel pinched by declining advertising revenues. The big corporation where he worked decided it no longer needed someone with Gene's income and talents. They decided not to launch any new publications. "This should have been my first warning my life was going to change forever," he said.

Luckily Gene had a good reputation and was able to find a new publishing job quickly. He moved to a smaller publishing company that served him well for a few more years. He knew his world was changing, but like most other males in their forties, he was in some type of denial. He was still making great money, he knew his business well, and he still wanted to ride the corporate gravy train.

When his biggest advertisers started shifting money into Internet marketing, he felt he had to make the shift with them and the market. He left publishing to pursue the Internet along with millions of others. And like millions of others, his dot-com crashed. He was broke, out of a job, and his 401(k) plan lost three-quarters of its value.

By October 2001, Gene and his wife had sold everything they had in San Diego and had moved to Las Vegas, intent on leaving life in Corporate America behind. They had fears, too, but were willing to take action to overcome them.

It took them only four months to find and acquire their first investment home in Las Vegas.

GENE'S EARLY REAL ESTATE DEALS

Gene didn't love the real estate game from the start. "The first house I bought was in Los Angeles. I bought at the wrong time. I overpaid. I had no idea what I was doing. I made such a bad decision, that in the end I had to do a short sale back to the bank. I just wanted to focus on my career as a magazine publisher. I thought, I'm too stupid to do real estate; I'm great at magazines. To make matters even worse, after losing $70,000 in the short sale to the bank, the federal government sent me a 1099 form for the same $70,000 (they claim that forgiven debt is income). I started to dislike real estate.

"The next home my wife and I bought was a little condo in the Bay Area . . . on *landfill*. I found out later no one would even talk to us because we lived on top of a garbage dump. I hadn't researched my real estate acquisitions. I was bad at it. By now I *loathed* real estate.

"Real estate was not working for me. I put the little condo in the Bay Area up for sale. It sold quickly, and I cleared $350,000 in profit. This was a turning point in my life. I went, 'Ohhhhh. I get it. One transaction generates $350,000. I've got to learn how to do this.' That's when my wife gave me Dolf's book *Real Estate Riches* and said, 'You ought to read this.'

"I didn't know anything about real estate, but I had experience in sales. Dolf had written, 'Look at 100 properties, make offers on 10, try to get 3 accepted, and then arrange finance to hopefully buy at least 1.' I had the discipline from my sales career to do that more than anyone else, because I'm willing to put in the time. With Dolf's blueprint, his REAP analysis software, and an intense desire to succeed, I went for it."

Since turning up at Dolf's San Diego event, Gene kept coming to more, convinced that he would learn a bit more each time. At one event, Dolf invited Gene up on stage to talk to the audience about his experience getting started in Las Vegas. Gene's enthusiasm was infectious. And his experience was inspiring. At another event, Gene showed Dolf a photo on his personal digital assistant (PDA) of his latest acquisition. "What do you think?" asked Gene, to which Dolf replied, "Looks like a standard Vegas house to me. What did you pay for it?" To which Gene replied, "A dollar."

As Dolf relates, "This was a turning point in the way I saw Gene. His enthusiasm and dedication were one thing, but there are plenty of people out there who feign both just to hang with you and hopefully ride off your skills, time, or money. But Gene not only was doing multiple deals beyond what most people would even attempt based on credit or cash reserves, but he was managing to pick up entire properties for one dollar."

"Okay," Dolf said to Gene, "it's time I go up and see what you are doing."

Dolf went to Las Vegas within a week. Gene's techniques were simple and effective. They decided to do some deals together.

Throughout his real estate teaching career, Dolf had always been dismayed at the number of people who, on hearing details of one of his deals, would dismiss it with a cursory, "Well, that's just a one-off deal," or "You just got lucky," or more incredibly, "You got that deal only because someone wants to sell you something, even at a discount, just so they can say they have done a deal with you."

Seeing an opportunity to show audiences that great deals are not one-offs, but can be found again and again, and enthused by the deals that Gene had already put together, Dolf said, "How about if we buy one house a week for an entire year?"

"When Dolf first suggested a house a week for a year, I was petrified," relates Gene. "The idea was overwhelming, but I was too scared to say no. I couldn't say no to my mentor. After all, if he suggested it, he must have thought it through."

Says Dolf, "I had said it on a whim without thinking it through too much, and had started to regret it as a harebrained idea that would require way too much effort, but seeing the enthusiasm in Gene's response made me feel I couldn't back out. If only I knew then what he had really been thinking!"

After discussing it at some length, they decided the idea had merit. Hopefully, it would make people believe that the formula could be replicated and that it was not dependent on being Dolf or Gene.

"Everyone wants to feel that they will be financially free," said Dolf. "We decided that by showing we could buy a home a week for an entire year, the average American could perhaps believe that they could at least buy 1 home a year for the next 10 years and become financially free in the process. Many people do not even believe that they can even buy income property. They think they don't know how, or that their credit is too bad, or that they don't have enough cash, or that it is too complicated. Sometimes they're just plain scared. We believed that if we could show people it is possible to buy 52 properties in quick succession, we'd convince them they could buy at least 1 home a year, and hopefully also inspire them to do so."

Chapter 2

WHAT WE DID IN VEGAS AND WHAT YOU CAN DO ANYWHERE

AN EXPLOSION OF AN EXPERIENCE

Fifty-two homes in fifty-two weeks. That's one home a week for an entire year. There were many ways to dissect the challenge we set ourselves, but time dominated everything. The pressure of buying 52 homes in 52 weeks was more intense than we could imagine. We had to see a lot of homes—kiss a lot of frogs. There were times when we said, "Can we just do three?" or "Can't we just stop now? Why are we doing this, anyway?"

Dolf told Gene he couldn't run up to Las Vegas from Phoenix (where he lived) five days a week. "It's not because I'm not willing to work that hard, but I already put in a long day down here," Dolf said. "Anyway, you will learn this game faster and better if you get in there on your own, discover the obstacles, and figure out solutions for yourself." Dolf adds, "Of course I always provided advice and support. But Gene was my legs and arms and ears and eyes and mouthpiece. I didn't have the time to do it. I couldn't have done it without Gene. It wouldn't have happened without him. And he wasn't about to do it on his own. We had a perfect symbiotic relationship."

The work took place all hours of the day and night. Sometimes people called at midnight getting off their shift at a casino, and Gene got out of bed to drive over to buy their house. He kept boxes of cashiers checks and documents in his trunk. If they were ready to sign over the deed to their property, he didn't care what time it was.

One house was acquired over the phone while Gene was in California, Dolf was in Australia, and the seller was on vacation in New Zealand. Phones rang at all hours of the day and night in two hemispheres and three countries. At times it was surreal.

For Gene it was a numbers game. He came from sales. "I can look at a hundred properties," he said. "We'd look at a hundred homes. We'd make offers on ten. If three were accepted, we'd hopefully end up getting one. Sometimes we'd go weeks without getting any, and once we got three in a single afternoon."

And it was a bizarre experience, too. Every week situations arose that seemed more appropriate to B-grade movies than real-life real estate. It was a big, sprawling explosion of an experience that conformed to nothing else we had ever been through. It was a view of life itself seen from a new and eye-popping perspective. We had a couple who weighed at least 300 pounds each who cracked a roof. We had a blackjack dealer's wife who assaulted a federal agent in a shopping mall. We had tenants who flew in from Los Angeles, partied all night for a week, and threw condoms on the neighbors' cars. We bought a house with a 1972 Trans Am in the garage that the sellers insisted went with the house. We used a private investigator who worked for Elvis and Sinatra, drove a black Chevy Caprice with tinted windows and a spotlight, and had a TV show based on his life. We had an old veteran with cancer who just wanted to die in his own home. We had a single mom who wanted a house in the neighborhood where her children's friends lived—and who would do almost anything to get it. Moves, divorces, births, bankruptcies, marriages, deaths, hopes, dreams, and nightmares. It was a learning experience, some of it crazy, and some of it straightforward. However, with each deal, we learned something and made improvements to our strategies that helped us with subsequent deals.

We bought model homes, pre-foreclosures, owner-carries, tax liens, quit-claims, and even homes on conventional loans using our own money for the down payment. We negotiated in Burger Kings and signed deals in Starbucks. We handed out business cards to cocktail waitresses, pool cleaners, and even a cop who pulled us over one day. We evicted deadbeats who changed oil in the living room and kicked holes in the walls. We helped good people with bad credit achieve the American Dream, people who happily live in those same homes, *their own homes*, today.

This began both as a challenge to ourselves and a quest to prove to others they can do it, too. It was fun, it was maddening, and it was profitable. Most important of all, though, while it wasn't always easy, it was possible.

And it's possible for you, too. However, you don't need to buy 52 homes in 1 year. You can buy a house a month, or a house a year for the next 10 years. You, too, can create wealth through real estate and be financially free.

WHY WE CHOSE LAS VEGAS

The real Las Vegas jackpots are not in the casinos, but in the suburbs. The astounding housing boom in the nation's

15

fastest-growing city had been going on for eight years, and was and is set to continue despite temporary slowdowns. A low cost of living, low taxes, warm climate, great food and entertainment, and newcomers pouring in from all over the country but especially California and the Midwest have fueled consecutive years of record growth.

The explosive market Dolf had been predicting for six years surpassed even his expectations. Population growth and land restrictions—factors Dolf cited during those six years that would drive the boom—met to create a superheated real estate climate. Las Vegas was and still is the fastest-growing metropolitan area in the country, with a population swollen from about 500,000 in 1985 to 1.6 million currently. Projections call for about two million residents by 2010. About 7,000 people move to Las Vegas each month.

Land is the other half of the equation. Las Vegas is surrounded by Native American reservations, Lake Mead to the east, mountains to the west, an Air Force base, and vast federal land holdings under the auspices of the Bureau of Land Management (BLM). Not only that, but for any land to be incorporated into the city, the transaction has to be approved through an act of Congress. In effect, the city is landlocked. They talk of the Manhattanization of Las Vegas. The number of high rises is already exploding. As available land disappears, remaining acreage grows more valuable.

Anecdotes about people buying a new home and having it valued at $50,000 more only three months later were common. One suburb that really took off was Summerlin, where Dolf and Gene bought many of their 52 homes. It is the area's largest development and the fastest-growing community in the country. When the 39-square-mile community is finished in 2020, it is estimated 80,000 homes will spread over 30 different village neighborhoods. Summerlin is located only 15 minutes from downtown Las Vegas, at the edge of the Spring Mountains.

But already, it is getting difficult to buy homes there now. Whereas it was easy to buy homes for less than $150,000 three years ago, today there is no inventory less than $300,000.

Are these prices driving away buyers? "Homes still look inexpensive to buyers coming from California, New York, and Illinois," one local home builder said.

What Made Las Vegas So Appealing

1. Every month, 7,000 people were moving into Las Vegas, and only 5,000 were moving out. That is a huge surplus that had to be housed.
2. Every day, 100 homes were being built, Saturdays and Sundays included.
3. Average capital growth when we started was around 12 percent—small in comparison with what happened, but way above the national average. And it was easy to beat this average just by choosing the right suburbs.
4. Wal-Mart, which spends millions a year deciding where to put new stores, went from no stores to 24 in five short years. *They* believed in the growth of Las Vegas.
5. The city is landlocked by mountains, Lake Mead, Native American reservations, Nellis Air Force Base, and BLM land. Unlike many other cities, land supply was severely limited.

We're not the only ones bullish on Vegas. Dennis Smith has heard similar stories time and again for the past few years. Smith is a housing analyst with 17 years' experience in Las Vegas and president of Home Builder's Research Inc.

Real estate gold-rush tales are "very true," he said. "I hear it time after time every day. It depends on the house, the price range, and the area. It's very difficult to generalize real estate, but it happens in all sectors of the market here. It's probably going to last as long as we don't have enough houses for all the people who want to move into them."

Climate, of course, draws new residents. Retirees are helping drive the market, with 18 percent of growth fueled by retirement housing. Property taxes are low, at about $1,000 per year for a $200,000 home. And, of course, Nevada doesn't have any state income tax.

A wave of casino and hotel construction was a big boost to the market in the late 1980s. The appearances of the Mirage, Excalibur, Treasure Island, MGM Grand, Luxor, Bellagio, Venetian, and more recently the Wynn are accompanied by ongoing housing booms. Which causes which is up for debate, but the fact remains that the proliferation of hotels has gone hand in hand with the housing boom. For many years the housing boom was evidenced by a proliferation of low-rise, single-family homes with stucco walls in desert sand colors, red-tile roofs, and large backyards with solid, six-foot-high fences. More recently, the trend has been condos or even multiple high-rise apartments.

"Industry is responding to demand," said Monica Caruso, director of public affairs for the Southern Nevada Homebuilder's Association. "In the last number of years it's been a response to population growth," Caruso said.

In 2002, new home sales at the 280 active subdivisions in the

Las Vegas area topped 22,500, twice the number sold in 1992. In 2004 experts predicted 27,000 new home sales—a record year for Clark County.

From July 2003 to July 2004, average capital appreciation in Las Vegas was 53.7 percent—an astounding figure. "I've never come across a statistic like that anywhere before," Dolf says.

"When we started, there were 7,000 people moving into Las Vegas every month, and only 5,000 people moving out. That represents a net inflow of 2,000 people per month, which is phenomenal. In fact, in Vegas they were building 100 homes a day, 7 days a week, just to accommodate the influx of people. You'd go to a suburb on four or five successive trips several weeks apart. On the first trip you'd see bulldozers preparing a subdivision for lots and putting in roads. On your second trip, they'd be putting in pads. On your third trip they'd be framing the house. On the fourth trip U-Hauls would be there moving people in. The rate of growth was spectacular."

The Vegas phenomenon is still booming at this moment. The great deals have not all been snapped up. Far from it; in November 2004, 12,500 homes were for sale in Las Vegas. Newcomers' numbers fluctuate, but approximately 1,500 people (net) presently arrive in Las Vegas every month needing a place to live. A glut of building has left a temporary oversupply, but remember that unlike the nation's second-hottest market, Phoenix, Las Vegas is landlocked. The city is becoming Manhattanized—the only direction to go is up. More than 50 high-rise condominiums are planned. Land will get scarcer and scarcer. One California developer and investor has spent $85 million on Las Vegas apartment buildings, predicting there will be another massive increase in value in three to five years.

Vegas was (and is) a great place for finding a motivated seller. With around 5,000 people leaving every month, chances are many of those 5,000 are leaving with odd circumstances to say the least. It made Las Vegas the perfect place for someone like Gene to learn a lot about real estate in a relatively short time. If he operated in an expensive place like San Diego, where he moved from, and made a mistake, it could have bankrupted him.

The most amazing thing about Las Vegas in 2002 was the investor world had not really discovered Vegas yet. Over the previous 20 years, Las Vegas had experienced only six percent growth per year. That was only three percent over inflation.

When Gene moved to Las Vegas right after September 11, 2001, the average *new* home was still only $150,000. It was a shock for him coming from the Bay Area and San Diego, where the average bad home—small and in a bad neighborhood—cost $380,000. When he saw new homes for $150,000, he thought, I can do this. . . . I can rent these for more than $1,000 per month. He looked at the risks and decided that even if he made a few mistakes (which he did), he wouldn't get wiped. He felt that he could handle a few payments if some properties were vacant. He couldn't understand why more people weren't rushing to Las Vegas.

Gene bought a home to live in on a private golf course for $190,000. The house is now worth more than $390,000. In California, homes were usually older than he was. Now he was in Las Vegas where an older home was 10 years old. He could not believe it! New! Never lived-in! Homes with new appliances, new floors, walls, and roofs, new everything, were available for $150,000.

While the statistics and anecdotal information on Las Vegas

can make it sound as though everyone should invest there, many towns and cities have their own unique combination of features and advantages that make investing in real estate advisable and worthwhile.

"The primary factor that will influence capital growth in real estate values," says Dolf, "is sustained population growth. And Las Vegas holds no monopoly on that. There are many regions in the country that are similarly experiencing notable population increases. The present population of the United States is estimated to be 296 million. Within one generation it is predicted to grow to 350 million, and by 2050 it is predicted to reach 380 million. Now population growth will not be the same throughout the nation; some regions will grow more than average, and others less. If you can correctly identify areas with higher than average growth, you will likely receive higher than average growth in real estate values."

But there are also other factors that can affect the growth of your investment destination, such as climate, the availability of work, whether there is a good high-tech infrastructure, access to markets (through road, rail, and air traffic), and susceptibility to disasters such as hurricanes, floods, earthquakes, and fires.

The beauty with real estate is that you do not have to be a rocket scientist to figure out which regions have higher than average growth. Trends in real estate are usually very slow to change, so past performance is generally a great indicator of future performance.

Bear in mind that you don't need to find the optimum city in which to invest. A profit of $100,000 made in the sixth-fastest-rising market in the United States is still a profit of $100,000.

Factors to Look for in Choosing an Investment Destination

1. *Population growth.* When all is said and done, if a city or town is losing residents (perhaps because the major industry closed down), then capital values are hardly likely to rise. Conversely, when there is a steady influx of people, capital values do go up. Monitor population trends (through the Internet, newspaper articles, chambers of commerce, etc.). Through the natural forces of supply and demand, a faster than average increase in population results in faster than average capital growth.

2. *Climate.* For decades and generations, domestic migration has tended to be from colder climates to warmer climates; hence the ongoing appeal of California, Nevada, and Arizona, for instance.

3. *Sustainable work.* For growth to be sustained, there has to be a diverse pool of work available.

Chapter 3

DETERMINING YOUR STRATEGY AND GETTING STARTED

STRATEGY

The most important thing in any endeavor is to have a plan. Without a plan, you don't really know where you are going and so will never get there. Even if you got there by chance, you wouldn't know it. People don't plan to fail; they just fail to plan.

Our plan was to acquire 52 homes in 52 weeks in Las Vegas. You may wish to choose a totally different geographic location, and you may plan on a different acquisition rate or final number of properties, but you must have a plan.

While a plan is necessary to achieve a goal, it is not the only thing you need. Las Vegas is the nation's fastest-growing city. It is also spread out. We couldn't run around the whole valley looking at houses at random. We had to narrow down our search geographically. We also had to determine which kinds of houses we wanted to buy; you cannot simply go after everything. You have to focus. To help us, we asked ourselves, What do most people want? Most people wanted three-bedroom, two-bathroom homes, or four-bedroom, three-bathroom homes. So that is what we decided to specialize in. We never, ever went outside our criteria. We didn't buy mansions with tiger cages and spas or ranches out on the outskirts of town. How many people want to rent a mansion with a tiger cage? No matter how tempting the deal was, we bought only three-bedroom, two-bathroom homes, or four-bedroom, three-bathroom homes.

Dolf and Gene's investing strategy focused on homes that didn't need any work. Since we were on a buying mission, we needed to find homes we could secure easily so we could move on to the next one. So, we narrowed it down to homes that weren't more than five years old. Homes that new wouldn't need a lot of work. Gene is not a handyman. (His wife banned him from even owning power tools so that he wouldn't hurt himself). Dolf, with his engineering background, has an affinity for fixing things, but his time is better spent doing other things. (Gene banned him from owning power tools so that he wouldn't waste time). Apart from that, the Las Vegas housing

How to Put Ideas into Action

1. Create a *Plan of Action*. Without a plan, you will never get there.
2. Determine and write down your *strategy* (you cannot look at every piece of real estate, so narrow the field down). See the sidebar Let's Talk Strategy and our Investment Strategy Worksheet as an example.
3. Stick to your strategy.

boom resulted in few tradesmen being available for small repair jobs.

Next, we needed to know where the best and highest appreciation was. We chose ZIP codes largely on the basis of their historical appreciation. You can often get that information from local newspapers, where they regularly update appreciation rates ZIP code by ZIP code. You can also get that information from a number of real estate companies, chambers of commerce, local real estate investor's associations, or on the Internet.

Once we had chosen our target areas, we set about creating marketing plans. We advertised what we wanted to do by

Developing Your Strategy

1. *Choose your geography.* Once you have chosen the city to work in, narrow the field down by suburb, ZIP code, or areas that have higher than average growth.
2. *Choose the type of property* you will invest in. Do you want older homes, with more established gardens and more maintenance requirements, or newer homes in outer suburbs with longer commutes?
3. *Choose your marketing plan* to attract potential properties. Will you pursue properties that others advertise, or will you advertise seeking properties? Which combination of flyers, newspaper advertisements, community notices, and real estate agents will you focus on?

Let's Talk Strategy

Before you put money into a deal, it's important to create a buying strategy. Then, you need to stay true to this plan. After all, how can other people help you find great deals, and how can you even describe what you're looking for if you don't know yourself?

We have created an outline for a simple investment strategy that will help you focus your plan of attack and assist your search for terrific deals. It's broken into the following segments:

Plan of Action
What is my goal and what is my plan to get there? We plan to acquire more than 52 homes this year. That's a lofty goal, but we purchase homes on a full-time basis in a very hot market, and are rather good at it.

Your plan of action may be to acquire two homes the first year, then one home a year for the next 10 years – a wonderful goal, one that is easy to accomplish and one that every person should be looking to do.

ZIP Codes
No matter what city you are investing in, you need to know which ZIP codes you want to focus on. Some investors refer to this as farm-area investing. It's a good way to focus your attention. Remember, a focused investor is a successful investor.

Since Gene lives in Las Vegas, he is very familiar with appreciating areas. If you are new to a town, or are not sure of the hot areas, go to the local chamber of commerce or a large real estate office to get this information.

Criteria
What types of properties do you want to focus on? We like to purchase single-family homes. We like three- or four-bedroom houses with two- or three-bathrooms and a two-car garage. We want newer homes in appreciating areas. We also like homes whose owners need to sell fast or are facing foreclosure. Our favorite: owners who will carry financing or agree to stay on the loan.

Financing
We buy 60 to 70 percent below market if the seller wants to sell for cash. Otherwise, our preferred method of buying homes is using the existing

financing. Our rule of thumb is to find homes that are 20 to 40 percent below market, with owner financing available.

Home Prices
This is very important for several reasons. We want to find homes the largest segment of the population will be interested in buying at a later date. The more expensive the home, the fewer number of people who will be able to qualify to rent it. In this type of economy, we look for homes ranging from $150,000 to $250,000.

In Las Vegas, the average price of a new home is $187,000. That number is extremely important to know and understand. By knowing the average cost of a new home and buying only average-priced homes, we know we can always keep our homes occupied.

Search
The easiest way to search for property is using the newspaper. We look for *For Sale By Owner* listings in our targeted ZIP codes that correspond with our financing guidelines. We have a buyer's agent realtor who searches the multiple listing service (MLS) to find *OWC* (Owner Will Carry), *Owner Financing, Facing Foreclosure, Must Sell, Moving, Transferred, Reduced, Desperate Seller, Make Offer or Fallen Out of Escrow.*

Additionally, we use the Web to look at FSBO (For Sale By Owner) sites, eBay Homes, Yahoo!, HUD Homes, sheriff's sales and tax liens.

No Interest
Sometimes it's better to tell people what you're not interested in so they don't waste your time. More importantly, it keeps you focused on what you want to buy and what your buying strategy is.

The types of properties we are not interested in are condos, town homes (this may change), mobile homes and homes more than 10 years old (keep in mind, this is Vegas). We are also not interested in large acreage or horse properties.

Needs
We are currently looking for other new investors to "bird dog" properties for us. We show them our

Let's Talk Strategy *(Continued)*

investment strategy and let them loose. Depending on the deals they find, we give them up to $1,000. (If you are worried they'll take the deal themselves, make it clear that you won't work with them again if you cannot trust them.)

We also list in our investment strategy we are searching for a very aggressive real estate agent who is not afraid to offend other agents with low offers. We need an agent willing to send out literally hundreds of offers.

Since the seller always pays the commission, a good seller's agent can help go through the multiple listing service and bring us good properties to consider.

It's imperative you do not rely on just one bird-dog investor or one type of seller's agent. Since the deal of the decade arrives every week, you need several people helping you find it.

Contact Information

Be sure to have several ways your bird dogs and buyer's agents can contact you. You should have a computer, e-mail, fax, cell phone with voicemail and a regular phone with a good voicemail system that you can access from anywhere in the world.

Got You Covered

We have a special memo we like to place at the end of our strategy documents:

"We are NOT interested in appraisals. Nor are we interested in the amount of 'upgrades' a seller claims to have made to a property.

Market value of a home is the price an individual would pay for that home today.

We expect that our agent will arrive at this number utilizing recent comps (within 3 to 6 months) with TIGHT criteria. This will be the ONLY acceptable form for calculating property value."

This way, there is no confusion if our agent or bird dog brings us homes that do not fit our criteria. We incorporate this type of format so when we do get something that fits our strategy, we don't hesitate to make an offer and make it "subject to" my partner's approval or "subject to" my inspector's final approval.

This is key. Do not wait to make an offer! The deal will be gone and so will your agent and bird dog. If you are serious, you must pull the trigger. Otherwise, you will be labeled a non-player and not get the best deals.

Our worksheet has given us the clarity to understand what we're looking for, what we'll pay and how we plan to buy it. We have never seen another investor use a tool like this, and we hope it will become the cornerstone of your investing.

Here's Our Plan

Investment Strategy Worksheet

Plan of Action

Purchase 25 to 35 homes in specific ZIP codes with good to excellent appreciation rates. This is a long-term hold strategy! We are NOT interested in flips.

ZIP Codes

89143, 89144, 89149, 89128, 89129, 89134, 89135, 89138, 89147, 89148, 89141

Criteria

3- or 4-bedroom/2- to 3-bath homes ONLY! 10 years old or newer. Pools OK. ***30% UNDER MARKET***

Financing

75% LTV or best case - subject to existing financing.

Home Prices

$150,000 to $250,000

Search

"OWC," "Facing Foreclosure," "Must Sell," "Reduced," "Desperate Seller."

No Interest

Condos, 2-bedroom homes, town homes, mobile homes, horse properties and homes more than 10 years old.

Need

A professional real estate buyer's agent who is aggressive and not afraid to offend other agents with low offers. You will be working with two seasoned investors. We expect the agent chosen to represent us by sending out literally hundreds of offers. However, we are SERIOUS about purchasing and controlling a minimum of 25 to 35 homes in the next six months.

Contact

Gene Burns - (555) 123-4567 (ofc), (555) 234-5678 (fax), (555) 345-6789 (cell), gburns@service.net, HIGHLY CONFIDENTIAL - if chosen to represent us, we EXPECT total privacy and confidentiality.

different means, adapting our strategies and tactics as we went, and learning along the way.

With our strategy in place, we set out to implement it. Part of our strategy was to find motivated sellers through flyers. So, we went to Kinko's and printed out simple one-page flyers saying variations of "I'll buy your house. Is your house a problem? Guaranteed closure in 24 hours."

Sample advertisement

I'LL BUY YOUR HOUSE—*FAST*

Here's Your Quick and Easy Solution

- **STOP FORECLOSURES.**

- **INSTANT CASH**

- **INSTANT debt relief.**

- **FREEDOM from maintenance hassles.**

- **GUARANTEED written offer within 48 hours.**

- **HARD-TO-SELL HOME? No problem!**

- **NO EQUITY? No problem!**

24-hour FREE Recorded Message
Toll-free: 1-800-555-1212 ext 3.

We had business cards printed with similar details on them. We tried the text on the back of our ordinary business cards, and separate cards with just the information.

Sample business card front

$500 REWARD!!!!

For information leading to my purchasing a home in your area.

Back

I BUY HOUSES—*FAST!!!!*

Call me if you know someone who needs help

Moving? Bad Tenants? Need Fast Cash?
Vacancies? Behind on Payments? Divorce?
Foreclosure? Estate Sale? Maintenance Problems?

Call 1-800-555-1212 ext 3—24 Hrs

Having lunch, we'd give our cards to the waiter or waitress and say, "Hey, if you know anybody who's about to lose their home, give us a call. If we get the house, we'll send you $500." People about to lose their home know other people, and they generally do not hang out with the Hearsts or Vanderbilts. What's more, if you offered a $500 finder's fee to a heart surgeon or trial lawyer, they would consider it demeaning and the rewards financially trivial to ask their friends if their house was in trouble. But to a waiter or waitress, $500 is the equivalent of miles of wandering around a restaurant being nice to picky diners.

We also put up signs on lampposts, community notice boards, and company staff notice boards where we could.

In all cases—flyers, business cards, posters, and notices—we listed a phone number with a recording.

One day, Gene found a pizza-flyer delivery guy who would deliver 10,000 flyers to homes in ZIP codes of our choosing for only $600. Within 24 hours of having these flyers delivered, we received 25 to 30 calls. Some calls were from people just wanting additional information. Others had homes outside our criteria in terms of age, size, or condition. Some were not really motivated to sell and were just checking to see if we'd pay $50,000 more than market for their home. But we ended up buying two or three homes. When we found out this worked, we started focusing more on the flyers.

We started seeing patterns and started honing in on things that worked. As the Las Vegas market heated up and more investors moved in, ads in newspapers became progressively less effective, and our flyers became more effective. By month three we knew what worked and what didn't work. The ploy of putting up signs on lampposts and trees generated less and less leads, and we abandoned this practice. The sign on our truck did not work well, either. As Gene says, "The low point of this ploy was someone phoning not to offer a property for sale, but to inquire who was the blonde in the passenger seat. Other times, the caller would say, "Whoever is driving truck so-and-so should be fired—he just cut me off!"

Of all the different things we tried—the signs, business cards, flyers—networking turned out to be the absolute best method. If you treat people fairly and ethically, word will get out that you are good guys and will do what you say you're going to do. It's also the cheapest way to find motivated sellers.

MOTIVATED SELLERS

Finding motivated sellers is one of the most important components to being a successful investor. If someone is not motivated to sell their home, you will probably never get a good deal from them.

New investors often assume that the list price of a house must be what the house is worth and consequently do not recognize a bargain when they stumble across it or realize a property is being offered at too high a price. Sometimes, people place their homes on the market at a high price just to test the market, on the basis that "everything is for sale at a price." A seller may have unrealistically high expectations as to what their property is worth. They may also be advised by well-intentioned friends or relatives who want to boost the seller's ego by telling them that the bright polka dots they so painstakingly placed on the walls make the house worth a fortune. They may also have fallen victim to less than scrupulous real estate agents who secured the listing by suggesting a sales price

Where Are the Motivated Sellers?

Did you know that as of mid-2005, there are two million homes going to foreclosure? There are lots of these deals, and they are not hard to find.

First and foremost, let everyone know you are a private investor. After all, if no one knows what you do, how can you expect anyone to bring you a deal? (And if you're embarrassed to be a real estate investor, maybe you should think about keeping your day job.)

Advertise that "We buy houses" and "We stop foreclosures." Put up signs and posters, and hand out business cards everywhere you go. Make flyers and door hangers, send postcards, and advertise in small community newspapers. Do dozens of things to let the world know that you buy real estate.

We receive a Notice of Default (NOD) list every day from a title company we do a lot of business with. We also receive lists from real estate agents.

As for the people on the NOD list, we call them, write them, send postcards, and leave notes on their doors. We also meet with neighbors to find out what's going on with properties. We even knock on the doors of houses in our target areas that have the most equity.

But our favorite way to find these people is to have them respond to our ads; we love it when they call us. Don't be afraid to advertise. Evaluate, measure, and change your ads if necessary. This is a business, and you will need to invest time and thought into it.

higher than other agents (or members of the buying public) will agree to.

However, just as there are many reasons why people will attempt to sell a property at much more than true market value, so there are many reasons why people will sell a property at less than true market value. Nearly all of these situations involve a motivated seller.

A motivated seller is someone who *must* sell the home. They can't afford to have the property on the market for eight months, or even eight weeks. Perhaps they haven't been able to sell it up until now, perhaps they cannot find a tenant for it, perhaps they cannot get anyone to list it (they have no equity to cover the commissions, for instance), or perhaps they are facing bank foreclosure because of the sheer weight of all their debt.

What causes people to fall into this quagmire? There are many reasons: divorce, job loss, economic slowdowns, medical problems, job transfers, armed services transfers, problems with drinking, drugs, or gambling, adjustable rate mortgages being switched from a low introductory rate to market interest rates, or just plain old spending beyond one's means (one of the most popular sports in this day and age).

Most of the motivated sellers we met were people who had simply spent more money than they had earned. Maybe they hoped they would cover their spending by getting better jobs, pay raises, inheritances, or richer and more benevolent relatives. Maybe they hoped they could keep borrowing against the increasing equity in the home. Most of them probably didn't even begin to figure out how they would pay for their spending; they simply had easy credit and used it. Currently more than 40 percent of Americans spend more money than they earn. When you add to that statistic the fact that more than 70 percent of Americans own a home, then there is a Perfect Storm scenario forming for the largest foreclosure calamity ever seen.

When people called us about helping them out of their situation, Gene always asked why they didn't sell it themselves or use a real estate agent. Every time they said they didn't have enough equity in the home to pay the agent's commission. Obviously no agent will list a home under those conditions. So the home owners were forced to try to sell the property themselves. They would run a small (cheap!) ad in the local paper and maybe put a (usually bad) FOR SALE sign in the front yard, or, even worse, in a front window. Fewer than 14 percent of home buyers look in newspapers! It's another important reason why you need to hire a real estate agent to list your property.

Most of the houses we inspected with a view to buying them were in reasonable to great condition. We wondered how the owners could have gotten behind in the payment. And then we would spot a spiffy new truck, or a monstrous plasma TV, or a fast boat, or a newly installed negative edge swimming pool. Somehow the owners never thought they were spending beyond their means, and it never occurred to them that they could pay the arrears in the mortgage if only they got rid of the toys. One seller in particular had a beautiful four-bedroom home in a desirable neighborhood. He was four months behind with the mortgage payments, and as we inspected the property, we saw a new dragster racing car in the garage, polished to a perfect shine. It had to be worth at least $80,000. And yet the home owner preferred to keep the dragster (which could only go down in value) and sell the house (which even he must have known would go up in value), rather than the other way around. This was one of the first properties we looked at.

Today, the increased value of his house would have enabled him to buy three dragsters and still have money left over, but he scoffed at the suggestion that he sell his dragster. (We did not buy his home as instant turf still had to be laid, and we couldn't be bothered with the effort.)

Many home owners, seeing values rise dramatically, immediately borrow against the new equity, thinking they can do this because they are now "richer." However, they forget two things. First, a larger loan means higher mortgage payments. Second, in the exuberance of rising house prices, owners often forget that as a consequence, property taxes can rise accordingly. This further dents their monthly cash flow.

When reality hits, it can hit fast and hard. Finances get rough. Marriages strain. Families start hating the home and the city that (in their minds) ruined their dreams. They can't wait to leave the stinking heat and critters and go back to where they came from before they embarked on their unfortunate Vegas experience. What really ruined their dreams was the desire to experience instant gratification. It's trying to impress people you don't know with money you don't have; a common American tragedy.

Let's take a closer look at three main reasons people become desperate to sell their homes: divorce, adjustable-rate mortgages, and addictions.

Many motivated sellers rise from the ranks of the newly-divorced. Anyone in love has faith in the couple's finances, and abilities to work through financial challenges together. However, in a divorce situation, many people are astounded to see a different side to the ex. Often, the most tempting solution is just to "sell the place as fast as possible, split the proceeds, and be done with it forever." Getting an ex out of one's hair usually takes priority over maximizing the sales price.

In the heat of anger and passion, either party may quitclaim their interest in the home to the other party, thinking they are harming them in some way. Once Gene heard a man tell his wife, "Here's the home! You deal with it! It's not my problem any more!" Nothing could be further from the truth.

What the man did was sign away all his rights to the home—any and all rights to enter it, share in any profits, or take part in decision making. The only thing he didn't sign away with the quitclaim was his financial responsibility to the bank or mortgage holder. The *only* way to get off the responsibility of the loan is to pay it off in *full*. When you quitclaim, you no longer co-own the home, but you are still co-responsible for the debt.

If your ex does not make the payments, and if the home goes into foreclosure, your credit will be affected even though you no longer have ownership in the home. The craziest (and worst) thing about this situation is that you have no power to sell the home to stop the foreclosure because you no longer own it. Your ex does.

Adjustable-rate mortgages and financial overextension have been the downfall of many home owners and have turned them into motivated sellers. Here's how the two factors sometimes spell disaster.

Buyers who have never experienced a downturn in the real estate market often want to buy a home in an area they really can't afford. Usually these buyers are younger. Mortgage brokers come along with products just about anyone can get. They use taglines like "NO MONEY DOWN, SPECIAL FINANCING." A typical product is a three-year adjustable rate mortgage (ARM). The interest rate is fixed for the first three years and then reverts to market interest rates. To qualify, applicants can use Stated Income, which does not require salary verification.

Of itself, the program is not bad, but both the bank and the borrowers assume that the real estate will appreciate significantly in the next three years. The buyers want the new home badly, but since they can't qualify for a conventional loan based on their joint income, they in essence stretch the truth on their loan documents stating they make more than they really do to qualify for the loan.

Often, the new owners using this type of loan can barely make the monthly payments on the three-year interest-only loan they signed up for, and even if they can, they are usually never prepared for additional costs like taxes, insurance, and homeowners association fees. Assuming they survive the first three years, however, the crunch comes at the end of year three, when interest rates revert to market rates. Even if they go up only one point, the owners are not prepared for the big increase in their monthly payments. Depending on whether the loan is tied to prime or LIBOR, their loan may adjust every month or every quarter. LIBOR is the London interbank offered rate, the interest rate offered by a specific group of London banks for U.S. dollar deposits. LIBOR is used as a base index for setting rates of some adjustable-rate financial instruments, including adjustable-rate mortgages.

The home owners barely have their heads above water, using all their credit cards to keep creditors at bay but still driving around in a big Hummer or SUV costing $50 a week to fill up with gas. Let's say their monthly payment is $1,800 on a $400,000 home. If the rate goes up just 1 percent (which it has in the past and could easily do again; when we were doing our deals, interest rates were at a 50-year low), the new payment could be as high as $2,133. If the rate went up 3 percent, the new payment would be $2,800. Like almost all other

Americans, the home owners may have no savings and often won't be able to afford the new payment. Add in any change in lifestyle (sickness, new baby, commission sales slowdown, lay-off, you name it—just life), the most important monthly payment may not be made.

Now what do they do? They'll try to refinance. However, many people have already pulled all the equity out of their home. (If they succeed in refinancing, the apparent reprieve is illusionary. While they have the capital to make monthly payments for a while, their monthly mortgage bill has now increased, so their cash flow is actually worse.) Maybe some can borrow from family, but that's not a long-term solution. Loans between family members are rare because they have a history of not being paid back on time or in full.

What usually happens is that they put the home on the market, along with hundreds of other people trapped in a similar situation. If there is no equity, they can't even hire a real estate agent to sell the home because there is not enough equity to pay the commission, which is typically 6 percent in most places.

By now they have become motivated sellers. This is when investors buy the homes from sellers who are sufficiently motivated that they are willing to stay on the loan and take very little money to get out from under crushing debt created by a lifestyle they could never really afford. This situation will continue to be a major problem for thousands and thousands of Americans who purchased using 3-, 5-, or 7-year ARMs. It's also going to be a major opportunity for investors.

Addictions are a third main reason people become desperate to sell their properties. These addictions may take the form of alcohol, other drugs, gambling, or just going out and spending large on credit cards. Las Vegas probably offers addicts more outlets for their compulsions than most other cities, but you will find people forced to sell their homes because of addictions in any city. Often these addicts are in a perpetual state of denial; they cannot see how their predilection for fast cars, or continual drinking, or whatever, is causing them to lose their home.

REAL ESTATE ACQUISITION PROGRAM (REAP)

Whenever Gene found a house, he used the Real Estate Acquisition Program, a software program Dolf created and developed, to see if the house was worth investigating further. REAP is a powerful property analysis tool enabling users to analyze the investment value of real estate.

After entering all the pertinent details of a property, including the purchase price, rental income, vacancy rate, property taxes, management fees, maintenance costs, homeowners association fees, and mortgage details, REAP generates seven reports (numeric as well as graphical) to provide an indication of how the property is likely to perform. The reports include details on the cash-on-cash returns (both before and after tax) and the internal rate of return.

"While REAP can absorb all the numeric data on a property such as purchase price and range, there are of course aspects of a property REAP cannot accommodate, like the look and feel of a place," Dolf says.

However, most of the decision of whether you should buy a piece of real estate should focus on the numbers. It's the numbers that count, not the feel of the place or whether the window

The REAP Program

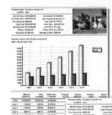

43

in the kitchen is positioned correctly relative to where the sun rises in wintertime. It is purely a numbers game.

- What does this property cost?
- How much cash will we have to put in?
- What are vacancy rates in this area?
- What are the rental levels?
- What are the management fees?
- How much are we paying for it?
- What should it appreciate to in the short term?

REAP does account for all the numeric data associated with that property, but because it can't take account of everything, you can't rely solely on REAP to make your decisions.

"A house that performs very well on REAP but is in the middle of an industrial park with no view and oil on the ground may be a worse deal than another property REAP doesn't evaluate highly on its own, but that is on top of a hill with a spectacular 360-degree view surrounded by BLM land," Dolf says. "However, once you look at a lot of properties through REAP, you will get a good feel for what works and what doesn't."

Of course some properties may work well for one investor, but not for another. For instance, if the investor has a lot of income, like a neurosurgeon who makes $800,000 per year, they can afford some negative cash flow in return for high capital growth. Someone with a low-paying job with a lot of expenses has to get investment property that generates high cash flow, and the price they'll pay is a slightly lower capital growth rate. REAP doesn't give you a yes or no decision. It is dependent on the individual circumstances of the investor and other factors you can't always quantify. However, when you are armed with a program like REAP, you can look at about 100 properties in a day, take a minute to analyze each one, and know which five or six you want to look at further.

"That's exactly how we used REAP in the challenge," Gene said. "It helped us figure out which properties were hot and which were not. After doing 30 or 40 REAP analyses, you know whether the deal is going to work or not. You get to know that the home here with the $1,000 mortgage will rent for $1,200 and that if it costs $5,000 to get in, you'll get your money back."

While our tools and criteria were sound and clear, our timing could not have been better as far as market conditions went. Dolf always says, "When things are good, they're bad, and when things are bad, they're good." It was just after 9/11 and air travel, hotel occupancies, and optimism were all down. In other words, market sentiment was down, and this created opportunities for Dolf and Gene. In any market at just about any time, there will always be factors that can make that market unattractive, such as natural disasters (hurricanes in Florida, floods in Mississippi, fires in Arizona, or earthquakes in California). The trick is to identify them and, often, to go against the grain.

Some people thought that Vegas was finished, but the majority of the people leaving for good were people who just wanted to be back close to their families. There is no real sense of community in Vegas. That struck even Gene, who grew up in Los Angeles, a city where no one is a native. "But at least in Los Angeles we all knew families in town and from church and the grammar schools and high schools," he said.

Everyone who moved to Las Vegas says the same thing: It's hard to meet people. The reason for this is the population is so transient. Locals who do call Vegas home are not eager to start relationships with new residents who are going to be in town for only a few months.

It was a perfect real estate storm: cheap new homes; motivated sellers; low-money deals; owners' emotional detachment from homes; and sparse investor competition.

Many people come to Las Vegas not for a resort, but as a last resort. "If you haven't made it anywhere else in the United States, this is your last hope," Gene said. Inexpensive housing and round-the-clock jobs suitable for the unskilled and uneducated draw blue-collar workers from across the country. About 85 percent of Las Vegas residents have no college education.

Partly as a result of that demographic, people who buy on a lease-option rarely exercise their option to buy the home, we found. The attitudes and opinions that got them into their situations (not having a cash deposit or sufficiently good credit to buy a home conventionally) have not changed. "The reason they have bad credit is because when they sign their name to things, it doesn't have any meaning to them," Gene said. "When they're late on payments, they're mad at everyone but themselves. However, they keep the places clean and tidy, as they still harbor the hope that one day they will exercise the option and own the property. The house means something to them."

WHAT IT TAKES TO SUCCEED

One of the top keys to our success was the willingness—and guts—to take action. He who hesitates is lost. If you sit around and think too much, the good deals will be snatched up by other investors who don't think as much. Always take things off the market. Our buyer's agent always had a bunch of checks from us for $1,000 to $5,000. We always had her fax a check to take a house off the market. That buys you 24 to 48 hours to decide whether you want it or not. You can always say you don't want to do it if you discover something untoward. However, don't sit there and say, "Should I do it or not? I don't know. This is so confusing."

"I wasn't afraid to pull the trigger, because I could always back out," Gene said. "Even if you can no longer back out, be willing to cut your losses. The less money you put into a deal, the less risk you have. If you have a $5,000 nonrefundable earnest money deposit but the deal is no longer good, walk away. If you're not willing to do that, you shouldn't be in the game."

But the commitment needed to pull off the challenge took a lot more than the courage to walk away from $5,000. This was a commitment that went beyond a simple concept of work. Think about how the Wright Brothers learned to fly: They fell out of the sky and crashed. A lot. Think about that again: The pitch in their stomachs as they fell toward the Carolina sand dunes again and again, out of control, splintered collarbones in their mind's eye. They had a lot of scary experiences without the certainty of success before they soared.

Dolf wanted to partner with Gene because Gene wasn't afraid to take to the sky again and again.

"I didn't team up with someone with no real estate experience to show that someone with no experience could do it," Dolf said. "I teamed up with Gene because he had enough enthusiasm that would compensate for a lack of experience. He went the extra mile. He worked seven days a week, month in and month out. After Gene moved to Las Vegas, dozens of my students, no doubt egged on by Gene's successes, relocated to

Vegas to work the real estate market, and all have done exceedingly well. But Gene is the first person I know of who, out of literally thousands of people whom I admonished, 'Vegas is the hottest market on this planet,' up and moved to Vegas. He came and worked the market hard. The results speak for themselves. I knew that his can-do attitude and his will-do attitude would carry him through. That's why I partnered with him."

COMMITMENT

As Dolf relates, "Gene had unstoppable dedication to the task of sourcing properties. One night we were driving from Las Vegas to Phoenix. It was pitch dark, with no street lights, no moon, and no traffic. We were minding our own business, telling stories and laughing, when we noticed these eerie blue lights. We stopped laughing somewhat when we realized they were the flashing lights of a highway patrol car coming up behind us. We pulled over and turned the interior lights on so that the officer could at least see us. Creeping up beside the vehicle, with his hand ominously near his hip, he shouted out, "You boys got any guns in there?" We assured him we hadn't, and he came up, demanded car registration, insurance papers, and a driver's license, and went back into his patrol car. It was January 21. After some time, Gene sighed that the officer must be writing up a ticket. I asked him why he had already come to that conclusion; we hadn't even been speeding. He replied that this was the third time that he had been stopped so far that year, and the previous two times the officer had come back almost immediately, whereas this time it was taking so long that he must be writing a ticket.

After what seemed like forever, the officer came back and said that everything seemed to be in order. Gene asked if he had been speeding. The officer replied no, but that several miles back, at a turnoff, there was a stop sign, and a stop sign means come to a complete stop, not almost a complete stop. Now had it been me, I would have thanked the officer and gone on my way. Not Gene. He thanked the officer and pulled out his business card stating "$500 reward for information leading to the acquisition of real estate," handed it to the officer, and invited him to claim his reward. That is dedication to the task at hand.

NOT ALL DEALS WORK

While it may appear from the successes we had (we did after all successfully buy 52 homes) that everything was easy and straightforward, we had our fair share of trials and tribulations.

With one house we looked at, the owner told Gene she owed $200,000 on it. After signing a contract to buy the property, we found out that she had taken out a second mortgage for $30,000 as well. In other words, she owed a total of $230,000. Gene called her and said, "I don't want to buy this with the extra debt."

"She had some mean guy call me and pretend he was her attorney," Gene said. "He said, 'Well, you signed this contract and in Nevada, if you sign your name, that's blood.' I thought, Oh my God, what have I gotten myself into?" It was scary. I'd never been sued before. We learned a lot in those early months about what to find out, what to insist on, and what to avoid. In this case, we learned to find out from the bank exactly what was owed on the property prior to accepting the seller's word and signing a contract.

We also learned how to approach people.

RESPECT FOR OTHERS

One of the hardest things to do is go into someone's home and say, "Hi, I'm Gene. I'm interested in buying your house. Could you show me around?" as an icebreaker. You're sometimes walking into tense situations. People are behind on their payments. They know that you know that. It's up to you to create instant rapport, to put them at ease. Don't promise them anything. Try to be a little reluctant. When you're dealing with men, you don't want to come in wearing a three-piece suit. That's why Gene drives a truck, so he's not pulling up in a BMW saying, "Hey man, you lose 'em, we buy 'em, sign here."

We treat people the way we would want to be treated in that situation and get them to open up. "Tell us what's going on here. I'm not sure we can help you, but if you tell us everything, at least we'll have a better idea of what we can and cannot do."

It's amazing. They'll tell things to a stranger they'd never tell to a friend. One guy's girlfriend moved to Reno. He wanted $10,000 to bring his credit cards current, and we'd take over the payments on his loan. This meant he would sign the deed over to us. We were the actual owners of the property, but, to help these people out, we required they stay on the loan.

This meant we wouldn't have to go to a bank to apply for a new loan. We would have to sign a binding legal agreement

I Found One! Now What?

Your initial contact will usually be by phone, so it's helpful to keep a few things in mind. Number one, be empathetic, and don't try to act slick or too professional. Always refer to the house as the problem, and never the person. Above all, do three things: Listen, listen, and listen.

By listening, you will be able to determine if the property fits your investment strategy. For example, if the house has a monthly holding cost of more than $3,000, it may not fit.

Once you've gotten the seller to talk for a while, find out a few things. Ask questions like:

- How old is the house?
- What is the first mortgage? How far is it behind?
- Does it have a second? Is it behind?
- Do you know what it will take to bring the loans current?
- Are there any other liens on the property?
- Who is on the title? A divorced spouse? Another family member? (Always check who is on the title before going to the home. You can get this information quickly from the County Recorder's Office.)
- What are you asking, and what is it appraised for?
- Are you currently in bankruptcy? Which type? Will the trustee let you sell the home?

If things sound like they are in sync with your strategy, set up a time to meet. Again, we like three-bedroom, two-bathroom homes in nice areas with loans costing under $1,000 per month. We can fill those in any economy.

stating that they would stay on the loan for, say, five years, we would bring the loan current (pay off the backlog), make the monthly payments, and pay off the loan at the end of the five-year period (or earlier if it suits us) in return for which they would have to leave the property right away. If it's a home we really want, we'll give them a percentage of the sale price. We *explain* to people how we make money.

When we closed the first deal, Gene showed the home owners *everything*. He showed them what both parties could and could not do. "I said, 'Look, I know this is my first deal, but if you're willing to take a risk with me, I'm willing to show you how I make my money. And I'll give you a percentage at the end.'" That's how he closed the deal.

There are some nice people in bad situations. If you make them part of the process, they'll be willing to work with you. Show them *everything*. Show them what you can and cannot do.

Chapter 4

OUR FIRST DEALS

There are many ways of finding suitable investment properties. One simple technique is to drive around target neighborhoods looking for likely prospects. Yellowed lawns and unkempt flowerbeds are a good sign someone's about to lose their house; they have already stopped taking care of it. There is always an annoyed neighbor who can be helpful. Listen to them complain, and then give them a business card and say, "We come in and help homes like that. We help get neighborhoods back together."

One of the most creative marketing techniques we came up with was the free pre-foreclosure seminar. We advertised it on fliers as a free workshop to teach people their rights under foreclosure. We took out a free meeting room at a branch library (we were offering a community service), and then found an attorney willing to donate his time. A mortgage broker with subprime loans and a real estate agent also attended.

People showed up with their paperwork. The attorney looked things over and generally told them they had to sell their homes and move out. The broker found out whether there was any equity in the properties. Gene told them if all else failed, he might buy the property. We picked up three or four houses like that.

We also took out an ad in the paper like everyone else. That was how we found Emerald Waters, the first of our 52 homes.

EVERYBODY WINS

Everyone has heard of a win-win situation, but few people really know how to turn a seemingly hopeless situation into a true win-win situation.

Gene had run advertisements in local Las Vegas newspapers saying "I help people with houses in trouble." One home owner called Gene and said, "What do you do? What's your program?"

"I really don't have a program," Gene said. "I help people sell their homes." Gene asked him about the property and what was happening.

The owner had co-signed on the house with his daughter to help her out. She had lived there with her boyfriend, but the relationship became increasingly acrimonious, and after a final argument, the daughter moved to California, leaving the by then ex-boyfriend in the house. The problem was that he was not paying any rent.

Gene arranged to meet the father at the house in a street called Emerald Waters. It was a fabulous property. It had four bedrooms, three bathrooms, a pool, a spa accented with Spanish painted tiles, and a spectacular view of the Las Vegas strip. The only negative was the boyfriend. He was there, was the size of a UPS truck, and loomed over them as if he knew that the continuation of his rent-free status was being determined. Gene said to the owner, "Why don't we go somewhere else?" and they drove to a Jack In The Box.

The owner explained that he owed $224,000 on the house, and that the mortgage payment was $2,000 each month. He couldn't sell the house because it hadn't appreciated, and there was no equity to cover the real estate agent's commission or closing costs. He couldn't get $2,000 a month in rent, even if the Incredible Hulk left. The owner was semiretired and would face bankruptcy if he had to put down $24,000 each year on top of his personal expenses.

Gene offered to lease it from him for $1,600 per month for two years, and to pay $1 for an option to buy it within two years for $235,000. This is referred to as a "lease-option"—a lease with an option to purchase. Further, Gene offered them a share of the profit if we managed to on-sell it (sell it to someone else).

The father agreed to pay $200 each month for two years, and the daughter agreed to put in the remaining $200. This way the mortgage would be covered.

They closed the deal at Gene's kitchen table, in the presence of a notary. The option was recorded against the property.

Two weeks later Gene rented the house to a family. The husband had a good job, but bad credit. He offered to rent the house for $1,675 a month for two years, and then buy it for $279,000 under a separate lease-option agreement.

Right away, on our first house, we'd built in a cash flow surplus of $75 a month and a profit of $44,000 in two years' time. We were off to a roaring start! We couldn't wait to find the next deal.

However, the cash flow and profit on this first property were dependent on our tenant not defaulting.

Sixty days prior to the expiration date of the tenant's option to buy, the tenant defaulted, and we were forced to evict him. Normally, when a party to a deal defaults, it spells disaster, and on the surface, our situation looked bleak. At best, we had lost our cash flow surplus, and we no longer had a profit of $44,000 built in. However, the market in Las Vegas was not just rising rapidly, it was raging ahead at a capital growth rate never seen before. We put the house on the market. Instead of selling the house for $279,000 as we would have had to under the terms of the lease-option agreement with the defaulting tenant, it sold within 10 days for $325,000.

It raises the question of why the tenant didn't pay two more months' rent, and then sell the property himself for an extra profit of $46,000 ($325,000 less his $279,000 cost). It is not as if the tenant forgot to pay the rent, and that we sneakily and rapaciously took advantage of his oversight. On the contrary, we wanted him to go ahead with the deal so that we could cash in on our $44,000 profit (the difference between our purchase price of $235,000 and our sale price to the tenant of $279,000). We were so scared of losing that deal that we phoned the tenant to tell him he was behind in his rent, and asked him to pay up. He got indignant that we should be asking for rental arrears, swore at us over the phone in a very unsavory manner, and refused to pay.

Of course our fear of having the whole deal fall to pieces turned to jubilation when we realized our extra windfall.

Gene called the father and daughter and said, "Hey, you're not going to believe this, but we sold your house. We want you to come out to the closing because we have a check for you."

Their profit from their sale price of $235,000, plus the 10 percent we promised them from our $90,000 profit ($325,000 less $235,000) resulted in their walking away with $18,000. They were over the moon. The father thought he was going to lose the home and that it would end up costing a bundle in the process. Instead, he was off the loan, the house was sold, his

---

SUMMARY—Emerald Waters

Source: Seller responded to an advertisement.

Formula: Sandwich lease-option.

Our lease-option agreement with the sellers

- **(a)** We pay $1,600 per month for two years.
- **(b)** We pay an option fee of $1.
- **(c)** We pay $235,000 at the end of two years.
- **(d)** We give the sellers a percentage of our profit.

Our lease-option agreement with our tenant-buyer

- **(a)** He pays us $1,675 per month in rent.
- **(b)** He pays us $5,000 as an option fee.
- **(b)** He may buy the property from us for $279,000 at the end of two years.

Monthly cash flow surplus: $75

Expected profit on exercising of both options: $279,000 – $235,000 or $44,000.

Actual profit realized: Sale price of $325,000 – $235,000 or $90,000, less 10 percent given to original seller ($9,000) plus option fee received of $5,000 (less option fee paid of $1!) or $85,999.

---

headache was gone, and he walked away with $18,000. It was money they never thought they would see.

"Everyone made money," Gene said. "Everyone won. I love this game!"

INSPIRING STEVE

After this, our very first deal, we thought it would be easy to buy 52 homes. However, *doing* the deal is relatively easy. *Finding* the homes is the challenging part. We had to scour newspapers, run ads, talk with dozens of people, and look at hundreds of properties to find one that met our strict criteria. For every home that was being sold below market value, there were dozens offered above market. It was really a numbers game.

One house was in an attractive, growing area we had targeted: Summerlin. It was a two-year-old, single-story three-bedroom home with a den, well-located next to an upscale mall under construction.

The owner was a computer programmer who used the house as his bachelor pad. When he became engaged, his fiancée wasn't interested in living in the house. He didn't have to sell it; he had plenty of equity in it and he'd made a down payment of about $40,000. He was also an excellent negotiator.

However, after the house had sat on the market too long for the owner's comfort, he called our ad line and left a voice message. Gene checked the messages every day. When people are in high-stress situations, they can't wait two or three days. Other investors are waiting in the wings.

The owner started by telling Gene he had a real estate agent who could sell the property in a hurry. Gene explained that we would be interested only if we could on-sell the property to a tenant-buyer. The owner responded that if we could fill it with a tenant-buyer before the agent could sell it, the deal was ours. Then he told Gene he wanted half the profits of any on-sale. Obviously we were not going to reach an agreement in an hour with him. However, he liked the idea of our taking over his payments, taking care of everything, and getting half the profit when the house sold.

Although he was a very tough negotiator, we ended up doing a lease-option for three years. We agreed to split the equity.

Filling a house on Milbank Avenue turned out to be a challenge. It took us close to three months to find a tenant-buyer, but they turned out to be one of our best tenants.

Dan Brown and his girlfriend Melissa, both in their mid-thirties, were looking for a house when they spotted our ad in the newspaper. Neither of them had good credit. Dan's ex-wife had ruined his score and Melissa worked on commission in sales. "But we're really good with paying our bills," Dan said.

Dan works in loss prevention and is also in the Air Force Reserve. He had moved to Las Vegas from Michigan in 1998 and loved it from the start. "I'm never moving," he said.

After they had chosen the house, we checked their credit. We knew it wouldn't be perfect, but we wanted to make sure they weren't felons. We called their employers to verify they had jobs, and they were in with a $6,000 deposit. Five thousand dollars bought the option to buy the house at the end of the lease. The remaining $1,000 paid the first month's rent.

"It was definitely well worth it," Dan said. "I couldn't have been in the house otherwise. It worked out great for us and Gene was very, very helpful. When I first met him, I thought he was just a salesman trying to get his money, because he's the

SUMMARY—Milbank Avenue

Source: Seller contacted us through our advertisements.

Formula: Sandwich lease-option.

Our lease-option agreement with the seller

(a) We pay $900 per month for three years.
(b) We pay $180,000 at the end of three years.
(c) We give the seller 50 percent of our profit if we on-sell.

Our lease-option agreement with our tenant-buyer

(a) He pays us $1,000 per month in rent.
(b) He pays us $5,000 as a nonrefundable option fee (but the $5,000 went toward the purchase price if he exercised the option).
(c) He may buy the property from us for $260,000 at the end of three years.

Monthly cash flow surplus: $100

Expected profit on exercising of both options: $260,000 – $180,000 or $70,000 less 50 percent to the original seller, leaving $35,000.

Actual profit realized: $35,000.

happiest guy in the world, but he did everything he said he was going to do, and he explained everything whenever we had a question. He was great. We go to the same gym and I see him there all the time."

Dan and Melissa always paid the rent five days early. We never had any problems with them. We did everything we could to help them to buy this property. Milbank's area has appreciated from 10 percent to 20 percent each year since we bought it.

Dan and Melissa bought the house for $260,000. About a year ago it appraised at $305,000. The neighbor's house—identical to Dan and Melissa's—appraised at $425,000 this year. "They're going up quickly in Summerlin," Dan said.

He and Melissa also have a plan. "We're going to do the same thing Gene and Dolf do," he said. "Once we have enough money saved, we're going to take a chance and find an investment home."

THE VETERAN WHO CAME HOME TO DIE

We advertised everywhere we could think of. Some advertisements ended up in the Nellis Air Force Base newspaper. A retired enlisted man we'll call Mr. Ellette had terminal cancer. The cancer center in Las Vegas was closing, so Ellette was moving to California. He needed someone to take over his house payments.

After some discussions with Mr. Ellette and his wife, we paid $5,000 and agreed to take over the monthly payments on his $180,000 mortgage (there was no equity in the house). It was a new home on a street called Dusty View, but in a bad area. Adjacent streets were rundown, and the nearest grocery store taught a big lesson.

"Always go to the grocery store where people will have to shop," Gene said. "It will give you a sense of the demographics. If it's a scary place, that's going to tell you a lot right there. . . . I did the deal and then went to the grocery store. And it was like, Oh my God, this is *way* too scary." It was definitely the wrong side of town.

The Ellettes moved to California, and a rotund and devout couple rented the Dusty View house. We desperately wanted to help them. They wanted to buy a lease-option, but had trouble coming up with the option fee. We worked out an agreement with them that they would rent it from us, and when they were able to come up with the $5,000 option fee, we would start the clock and run the option to buy.

However, they struggled to pay the rent each month, falling further and further behind. To protect our investment, we

How to Handle an Eviction (If Necessary)

1. Make sure you have everything leading up to the eviction in writing, especially the rental agreement.
2. Enlist the services of an eviction service.
3. Have the eviction service deliver a five-day pay-or-quit notice to the tenants.
4. If they have not paid within five days, have the eviction service organize for the necessary paperwork to be filled out at the local courthouse, getting a judge to authorize the eviction. The local sheriff then supervises the locking out of the tenants.

learned about evictions and how to put together a team. We learned what the eviction laws were and started the eviction process every time our tenants were late.

Every time they were late, we sent them a five-day pay-or-quit notice. If you've agreed for the tenant to pay on the first of the month and on the second you haven't received payment, you can send them one of these notices.

It's easier to do it with an eviction service, which costs around $40. They deliver the notice and the tenants have five days to come up with the rent and penalties. If they don't, you go back to the eviction service and for an additional $40, they do all of the paperwork and have the local sheriff lock out the tenants and give them 24 hours to move all of their furniture and effects from the home.

Despite the large number of pay-or-quit notices, however, we never had to evict them: They left voluntarily, after reneging on one month's rent and, as you may be guessing, trashing the place. Somehow—both of them weighed in the high 300-pound range—they had gotten up on the roof and cracked the ceiling in many places. We spent a couple of thousand dollars to get the house back into livable shape.

Meanwhile we had learned a lot about whom we would and would not rent to, and where we should and should not buy. Check out a neighborhood before you buy. Shop at the local store before you buy. Try to meet with the tenants at their existing home. At the very least check out their car, as the way most people keep the interiors of their cars is very similar to how they will keep your house. The signs were all there, but we stubbornly refused to see them.

Then out of the blue Mr. Ellette called us. He was in the last stages of terminal cancer and living in a horrible place. He wanted to come back to Vegas and have his last days in his former house. He and his wife initially asked to rent the house, but renting to someone who is still on the mortgage has severe consequences if he (or later his wife) default on the rent. It can be very difficult to evict someone who is your tenant but still on the mortgage. (This is why we never rented a home back to previous owners who had been in default and were still on the mortgage.)

Out of compassion for their situation, we agreed to sell them back their home. It had gone up some $30,000 in value, and while we knew they did not have $30,000, we did not feel inclined just to give it to them, when we could have sold the house there and then to an outsider for a cash profit of $30,000.

So we quitclaimed the property back to the Ellettes (this gave them full ownership again of the property), but (with their agreement) registered a $30,000 second deed of trust against it. This way if the Ellettes ever sold the house or transferred it to another person, we should get the $30,000 back.

They also owed Gene $100 per month for a $10,000 personal loan. Mr. Ellette had asked Gene for help in paying off a credit card. Gene had lent him the money from a self-directed individual retirement account he shared with his wife, protecting himself with a third deed of trust.

"That shows you what kind of person Gene is," Dolf said. "Gene goes beyond the call of duty to help out."

"I protected the $10,000 loan with a deed of trust," Gene said. "I have a partnership. You can't mistake kindness for weakness. If it was 10 grand to save his life, I would have given it, but it was 10 grand to pay off a Visa bill. They had bought stuff, and used it, and now it was my money that had paid for it."

While Gene helped out by lending the $10,000 and letting the Ellettes sit on the $30,000 until the house was sold, he also

---

SUMMARY—Dusty View

Source: Seller contacted us through our advertisement in the Nellis Air Force Base newspaper.

Formula: Bought subject to existing financing.

Our agreement with the seller: We paid $5,000 down and assumed responsibility for the $180,000 debt, even though the deed of trust remained in the seller's name.

Owing to the seller's circumstances, we deeded the house back to them, with a $30,000 second deed of trust (interest free) back to us. Mrs. Ellette still lives in the house, but if she ever sells, we will get the $30,000 back. While we could have realized $30,000 in cash long ago, we felt this was the right thing to do.

Expected profit on eventual sale of house: $30,000.

---

told them he wouldn't forgive them the debt if they missed payments.

One of the things we like about real estate is that you can put anything you like into a contract. Try that with stocks or bonds! Gene could lend $10,000 and give them the use of another $30,000, but he had it structured so that he could ultimately get the money back.

Ellette was like a lot of other guys in the military. He had worked hard his whole life, probably picking up his cancer somewhere overseas serving his country, but for one reason or another, he hadn't planned well. However, he died in his own house.

FOUR DOBERMANS AND A PRIVATE EYE

A couple we'll call the Brimlads called us and said they were moving back to Missouri. The owner left a message saying three or four other investors were interested in the house. Gene called Mr. Brimlad and asked him to describe the house. It was a three-bedroom, two-bathroom home a few years old. Gene said he wasn't going to compete for the business. If the owner wanted to deal with a professional, call back. Mr. Brimlad called back a few days later.

The house was in good shape, but the Brimlads owned four huge Doberman pinschers. Gene told them part of the deal was for them to clean up the yard.

We started off buying properties using lease-options. The advantage was that for a relatively small outlay (the option fee) you could control the property, and even make a cash flow profit on the rental (the difference between what we were paying in rent, and what we could collect). However, we soon realized the advantages of owning the properties we were buying. We didn't want to buy lease-options. When the time arrives to sell the house, the owner can say, "You made $100,000, and I didn't make anything; I'm not going to sell." That is a big problem with buying lease-options. Furthermore, if the lease-option owner doesn't cash the check, the contract is void. Apart from that, you still have to deal with the owner. If they refuse to sell, you end up with a legal battle. It was just simpler to buy the properties outright.

Real estate investment has a very steep learning curve, but if you know all the tricks, it's hard to be burned.

The Brimlads needed $5,000 to move back to Missouri. We did our due diligence. The title report indicated nothing encumbered the house. The bank said while $130,000 was owed, there had only been one late payment.

We still felt uncomfortable with the Brimlads. We wanted to have the property deeded to a land trust, with Gene as the trustee. We set up a power of attorney, authorization to release information, and every other document we thought we might need to protect our position, and then bought the house for $130,000.

As it turned out, we needed every one of those documents.

Gene showed up at the house the day the Brimlads moved back to Missouri with their $5,000 check. They left a garage full of junk. The carpet had to be replaced and the interior repainted. They also neglected to clean up the Doberman-fouled back yard.

We had a 24-hour notary on hand named Eddie LaRue. LaRue has been a private investigator in Las Vegas for decades, working for Elvis Presley, Frank Sinatra, Howard Hughes, and The Mob. LaRue was the model for Dan Tanna, the protagonist of a flashy 1970s TV show called *Vega$* about a snappy guy with a hot car and sexy assistants. LaRue drives a black Chevy Caprice with tinted windows and a spotlight.

However, reality can be vastly different from TV. That morning LaRue's job was to stop by a house with a back yard full of dog poo and notarize papers on the trunk of a car.

Advantages of a Land Trust

1. Protects the home from the bank calling the loan due (better known as protection from the "due-on-sale" clause.
2. Offers asset protection from spurious lawsuits.

Gene Burns' Checklist for Buying Subject to Using a Land Trust

1. Seller signs the "Binding Legal Agreement"
2. Determine if the Title Company will insure a Land Trust
   a. If not, transfer Property into an LLC
3. Have all documents notarized and recorded in the County Recorder's Office
4. Due Diligence
   a. Compare local rents vs. existing mortgage payments
   b. Run comps to determine value
   c. Order a Preliminary Title Report (PTR) to show encumbrances on Property
   d. Check for existence of current title insurance
   e. Obtain Authorization to Release Loan Information from Seller and fax to lender Confirm loan balances
   f. Check PTR for liens, taxes due or Homeowners Association assessments
   g. Do a records check to see if any judgments have been attached to the Property
   h. Ask if there has been any work by licensed contractors on the Property during the previous ninety days (potential Mechanic's Liens)
   i. Arrange for a professional home inspection
   j. If possible, obtain original loan documents. These should include:
      i. Closing Statement
      ii. Promissory Note
      iii. Deed of Trust/Mortgage
      iv. Title Insurance Policy
      v. Copy of recorded Deed
5. Future Financing Obstacles
   a. Stay in contact with Seller if signatures on future documents or transfers are required
   b. Seller must attend closing at title or escrow that will allow for title insurance to be issued on the Property
   c. Banks will not finance properties without continuous title insurance and future conveyance of Property may also depend upon the continuous existence of title insurance
6. Closing Issues
   a. Put original "Binding Legal Agreement" in closing documents
   b. Conduct closing at Title Company
   c. Have Seller deed property into the name of the newly formed LLC
   d. Designate LLC as Trustee of the Land Trust and Seller as Beneficiary of the Trust
   e. Use the correct deeds for your jurisdiction. Consult with legal counsel if necessary. Deeds and other conveyance documents must be notarized
   f. Seller executes the Assignment of Beneficial Interest in Land Trust in favor of Investor
   g. Seller executes Due on Sale Disclosure Addendum
   h. Arrange for Renter's insurance and name Seller as additional insured
   i. Utilize Authorization to Release Information to obtain payment coupons, etc. from lender
   j. Change the locks and garage door codes
   k. Have title company record deed; do not record Assignment of Beneficial Interest

The documents LaRue notarized included land trust documents. The advantages of a land trust over a limited liability company (LLC) include preserving loans with great terms you don't want the bank to call due. Trusts are powerful tools that can also protect you from lawsuits.

Within a year Gene received a call from a federal bankruptcy trustee, "one of the scariest things that's happened to me."

The federal trustee asked Gene if he was the trustee of the land trust for the house on Rocky Bluff, and then told him the Brimlads were getting divorced and filing Chapter 7 bankruptcy, which is total liquidation of all assets.

"If we hadn't had the house in a land trust, the federal trustee could have called the loan due (by invoking the due-on-sale clause) or otherwise have forced the sale of the house

---

SUMMARY—Rocky Bluff

Source: Seller contacted us through our advertisement in a Sunday newspaper.

Formula: Bought subject to existing financing in a land trust.

Our agreement with the seller: We paid $5,000 down, and assumed responsibility for the $120,000 debt.

We then lease-optioned the property for two years, with an exercise price of $165,000. The monthly cash flow surplus was $100.

Profit on sale of house: $45,000.

---

to satisfy the bankruptcy. The trust owned the property, and because payments had never been missed, the house couldn't be touched.

In a Chapter 7 bankruptcy, all assets are liquidated to pay creditors. Since the Brimlads' names were still on the loan, in the eyes of the court, it looked like they had put the home in the trust.

Gene faxed the trust to the judge. This worked. The federal officials wanted to see that we were real people and that the trust was intact. The Brimlads had promised in the contract they would call us if they ran into financial problems. They never did. Even though they still had their name tied to the loan, they couldn't liquidate it.

Tenant buyers (a teacher and a water company employee) bought the house and did some wonderful improvements to it.

This was one of our best deals. We acquired the property for $120,000, which was what was owed on it. When we took over the loan, we had it appraised. The appraisal came back at $150,000. We sold it to our tenant buyers for $165,000. It will probably appraise soon at $180,000.

The best course to take in investment is patience.

THREE BEDS, TWO BATHS, ONE TRANS AM

The Dieras, we'll call them, decided they didn't like Las Vegas and wanted to move back east. "They just didn't like our Las Vegas lifestyle," Gene diplomatically puts it. When Gene arrived to look at the house, he noticed one of our flyers on their coffee table. "We hadn't targeted the area in our market research, but the Dieras' son had brought them the flyer."

Documents to Carry—Always

Samples of these documents are in the Appendixes at the back of this book.

1. *Authorization to Release Loan Information.* No matter what a home owner tells you about how much they owe on the property, always check this out with their bank. You cannot simply call the bank and get these details. The bank must have written evidence that the home owner is happy for this information to be released. The document that secures the release of information is called the Authorization to Release Loan Information. Have the owner fill it out and sign it, and you can then fax it to the bank and gain access to all the pertinent information. A sample Authorization to Release Loan Information document is included in the Appendix.

2. *Deed.* On the off-chance that the owners want to deed you the property there and then, have a Deed available.

3. *Limited Power of Attorney.* With the sellers moving back out of state, it pays to have a power of attorney to enable you to do simple things like turn on the water.

4. *Binding legal agreement.* This document covers what is being agreed to so that everyone has clarity going into the deal.

73

The Dieras didn't have any equity in the house because they had just bought it. "The people here aren't friendly," they told Gene. "There's nothing for us to do, and it's getting super hot. We just want to get the heck out of here."

"If you can get out by next month, my partner and I will make your next payment," Gene said.

Their faces lit up.

"You'll have to trust us to make the payments for the next three years," Gene explained, "as well as deed us the house."

"Where do we sign?"

We always carry an array of documents in the car ready to be signed. Power of attorneys, authorization to release loan information, quitclaim/warranty deeds, and others. Gene called Eddie LaRue to drive over and notarize the papers.

After they had gone back to Missouri, we did an inspection of the property. They had left it in spotless condition. The only problem was that they had left a 1972 Trans Am in the garage. We contacted the Dieras to find out when they were going to collect it, and the answer was essentially "We're not." When they went back to Missouri, they each drove a U-Haul with their other two cars towed. The Trans Am wasn't worth the cost of collection to them. We did have a spat over who should get the car. Dolf kept saying, "You have it," and Gene kept saying, "No, it's your car as much as mine; you have it."

Meanwhile, we were starting to feed our machine. Our fliers were working, and we made them bigger. Networking heated up, too. Deals of the decade came along about once a week.

We lease-optioned the house for two years to a nice retired military couple. He had been a Marine, and she had been in the Navy. We liked them, even though they were tough negotiators.

Larry Holiwell and his wife had been living in an apart-

SUMMARY—White Quail

Source: Flyers distributed to houses.

Formula: Bought subject to existing financing.

Our agreement with the seller: We assumed responsibility for the $133,000 debt.

We then lease-optioned the property for two years, with an exercise price of $153,000. The monthly cash flow surplus was $80.

Profit on sale of house: $20,000.

---

ment in Las Vegas. He was a retired Marine and Greyhound Bus driver. Their daughter's husband, a San Diego Marine, received orders to go to Iraq. Larry and his wife went and lived in San Diego for seven months to help with their two grandchildren.

When the Holiwells returned to Las Vegas, they began looking for a house. He had some credit issues he needed to clean up. While Larry was house hunting, he saw our ad and called. He looked at our ex-Trans Am house on a street called White Quail and liked the premium corner lot.

Larry paid Gene a deposit of $1,000 to take the house off the market. Within 30 days, he then paid the first month's rent, and an option fee of $4,000 for a two-year lease option. The option exercise price on the house was agreed at $153,000.

"There are some people who come into your life whom you want to help," Gene said. "We didn't make a lot of money, but we changed someone's life." They had had bad experiences with rent-to-own people. Gene took them down to the bank, and did a lot of work with them. They put $4,000 down, bought the house, and happily live in it today.

"They had some credit issues, but they got a piece of the American Dream," Gene said. "And we earned about $20,000 profit from that deal."

THE BLACKJACK DEALER'S WIFE AND THE FEDERAL AGENT

The house on Anchor Drive taught us many lessons, including to trust our gut feeling. The deal was one of our most bizarre. It was being sold by a Mr. Hamia, who had come to Las Vegas from Canada, bought about 30 homes, and promptly cheated a lot of people. Warrants went out for his arrest. Of course at the time we did not know this. Apparently the authorities are still looking for this guy.

He called Gene and said he wanted to sell a house. It was a three-bedroom, two-bathroom house with a swimming pool and big trees in the front yard. Hamia told Gene it was his primary residence, not an investment.

Gene looked at it. The house itself was great, but Hamia wanted an outrageous price for it, which Gene rejected.

Weeks later, Gene received an e-mail from Hamia, who was vacationing in New Zealand. He had found someone else to buy his house, but the deal had fallen through when the financing bank found out there was a *lis pendens* on the property, which is a lien on a property notifying the public that there is a pending legal action involving the property. Hamia said his ex-wife's husband had filed the *lis pendens*. Until the lien was removed, the house couldn't go into escrow.

Now Hamia was two or three months behind on the payments. He claimed he just wanted to save his credit. Hamia offered to deed us the property if we brought the loan current. He was in New Zealand. Dolf was in Australia. Gene was in California.

Gene told Dolf that there was a *lis pendens* on the house. He had no idea what it entailed, but he thought he could get it removed. If he could, the house was great and in good shape. It would be an interesting exercise, he added.

"Go for it," Dolf said.

We paid Hamia $6,000 for the property. He deeded the house to his fiancée, who signed it into a land trust in our name.

With the loan current, we lease-optioned the house in a month and a half to a blackjack dealer and his wife. They put down $7,000 as the option payment and the first month's rent.

During their second week in the house, a man showed up at the door. He told the blackjack dealer he owned the house, and he would take the rent. The blackjack dealer turned on his computer, looked up ownership on the county assessor's web site, and told the man to get lost.

Hamia and his ex-wife had been investment partners in a group of homes. After their divorce, she remarried and became business partners with her new husband, Mr. Ifield. Not long thereafter the new Mrs. Ifield died. Ifield claimed all his late wife's houses as his own. He was a closet cowboy lawyer who knew enough to slap *lis pendens* on everything. He was also sue-happy, and Gene was in his crosshairs.

Gene pointed out to Ifield that his name wasn't on any of the deeds or loans. "Why do you think you have a claim to this house?" Gene asked. He explained if the court proved the house was Ifield's, he'd get it back. In the meantime, he told Ifield to stop scaring the blackjack dealer and his wife.

Our attorney warned Ifield to stay away from the property, and then we began work on removing the *lis pendens*. We filed a quiet title action, which involves taking out a legal advertisement in the newspaper. It asked anyone with any claim to the property to come to court on a certain date and explain their side to a judge, who would then make a ruling on rightful ownership.

Ifield stopped bothering Gene. When we asked the judge to release the *lis pendens*, he simply said, "Sure."

We may have had the ex-owner's late wife's new husband off our backs, but we had challenges with the tenants, too.

SUMMARY—Anchor Drive

Source: Flyers distributed to houses.

Formula: Bought subject to existing financing.

Our agreement with the seller: We paid $6,000 to take over the debt of $150,000. We had sold it as a lease-option (with an option fee of $7,000) for a projected profit of $45,000, but the lease-option fell over, and we sold the property on the open market for $250,000.

Profit on sale of house: $100,000.

The blackjack dealer's wife was at the mall when a man bumped into her daughter. She got angry and hit the stranger with her purse, who turned out to be a federal agent. This earned her a three-year prison sentence for attacking a federal agent. The blackjack dealer couldn't make the payments by himself.

The property manager called Gene and told him the payment was 40 days late. When Gene drove over to the house, it was empty. He tiptoed in. "There was no one in there with a gun, and that's always a good thing." Other than a few holes in the walls, the house was in good condition.

That was in June 2004, when the Las Vegas market peaked and homes routinely sold above asking prices. We decided to sell Anchor Drive. We owed $150,000 on the house. If the blackjack dealer had gone to term on the lease-option, we would have made $45,000 profit. Instead we sold it in four days for $250,000, making $100,000 profit.

The lesson here is do the due diligence on the property, but don't be afraid of mechanic's liens or *lis pendens* if you can understand the merits of the claim. These can usually be easily settled. In the case of Anchor Drive, there was a lot of equity in the property, the loan was at a great interest rate, and the mortgage had a term of 15 years with 10 remaining. It turned out to be a great deal.

Chapter 5

LEARNING TO ASK FOR HELP

We started off our quest to buy 52 homes in 52 weeks by doing everything ourselves. We began to realize, however, that enlisting the help of others made a lot of sense, be it sourcing properties, doing due diligence, or any other part of the deal.

THE BEAUTIFUL GIRL AND THE PRIVATE EYE

A beautiful girl walks into a private eye's office and asks for a favor. It sounds like a movie, but that's how the story of our home on Blue View begins.

Our private investigator friend Eddie LaRue was in his office one day when the daughter of a friend stopped in to see him. She was in a divorce and needed advice. Laura, we'll call her, wanted her estranged husband out of the house and off the deed, so she could sell it.

LaRue recommended Gene and gave him a call. Gene looked at the house; it was beautiful. Laura convinced her husband to sign a quit-claim deed. He left. She wanted to keep the house but couldn't make the payments.

Laura wanted to save her credit, so she offered to leave if we would take over the loan payments; she was only one month behind. She deeded the property over to us, subject to the existing financing. Bear in mind that at the time, interest rates were at their lowest ever; homes could be refinanced at 4.8 percent. We acquired a $163,000 home simply by agreeing to take over the mortgage payments (plus the debt, of course). We lease-optioned it in no time for an option fee of $5,000 to great tenants who never bothered us. They have since exercised their option and bought the property for $208,000, giving us a profit of $45,000.

Blue View was the first time someone else brought us a deal. We'd promised $500 as a finder's fee, and we promptly wrote a check to Eddie.

SUMMARY—Blue View

Source: Referral from our private investigator.

Formula: Bought subject to existing financing.

The seller could not afford to keep the house, and we acquired it by agreeing to take over the existing mortgage payments. We lease-optioned the property for an option fee of $5,000 and sold it for $208,000.

Profit on sale of house: $45,000.

HIRE A TITLE AGENT

Tahiti Isle was a great house, in a great neighborhood. It belonged to a nurse who had developed carpal tunnel syndrome and couldn't work at the hospital any more. She couldn't make the payments, so she quit-claimed the house to her son, who lived with her. When the son divorced, he couldn't make the payments either.

They thought that the monthly payment was $1,200 and that the outstanding debt was $142,000. When we met them and inspected the house, we had them sign an Authorization to Release Loan Information (see Appendix A). We called the bank. It turned out that the monthly payment was actually $1,400 and the debt was in fact $148,000. Whether the inaccurate figures were intentional or just a result of the turmoil of their lives at the time is secondary to the observation that it pays to always do your due diligence.

Gene felt confident he could interpret the title report and didn't need to pay a title company to do something so trivial. With real estate, it pays to do your due diligence on *all* aspects of the transaction. All payments appeared up to date. However, we discovered after we had bought the property that while property taxes had been paid for the current year and the year prior, the property taxes for the year prior to that were still in default. The amount involved was a hefty $5,000. The house was headed for a tax lien sale, and we discovered this only after we had acquired the property. We had no alternative but to pay the $5,000.

One lesson from Tahiti Isle was to always hire a title agent to read title reports. They're very difficult to read, and, like any other document in any profession, chock-full of acronyms and

---

Title Agents

Always hire a title agent to read title reports. Your time is better spent looking for more deals, and the title agents know more about the subject than you probably do, anyway.

---

jargon. If you're putting money into a deal, you want to make sure there's nothing encumbering the property.

The owner wanted $5,000, and he wanted to stay in the house through Christmas. We agreed.

Filling Tahiti Isle wasn't easy, even though it was in great condition. We tried open houses, flyers, advertising, and putting it on our web site. People considered North Las Vegas to be not so desirable, even though it was perfectly safe. After the house had been 70 days on the market, we considered doing a Section Eight (government subsidized rental) just to get the property tenanted. Finally we went to our buyer's agent and requested she put it on the Multiple Listing Service (MLS) stating that we would be willing to sell it as a lease-option.

Before long, a real estate agent from California decided to take on a lease-option from us (he had never done one before). We had to pay a one percent commission up front to the agent who brought us the deal. However, since we hadn't had any success filling the property ourselves, we were more than willing to pay.

But you learn from every experience. The one percent fee is not on the option payment, or even one year's rental, but on the entire sale price should the tenant exercise his option. In

---

SUMMARY—Tahiti Isle

Source: Seller responded to flyer.

Formula: Bought subject to existing financing and sold as a lease-option.

Purchased for: $153,000.

Sold for: $180,000.

Costs: $1,800 in commissions, $5,000 in property taxes.

Collected: $5,000 option fee.

Profit on sale of house: $25,200.

---

other words, a home worth $200,000 today, but with an exercise price of $280,000, would attract a commission of $2,800 today. Given that most lease-options do not go through to eventual sale, this seemed a bit rich to us. So from there on in, we offered a flat $1,000 finder's fee for agents bringing us a lease-option buyer.

FIRE AND WATER

We bought Heatherwood for $150,000. It had a hidden second mortgage for $20,000, which the owner hadn't disclosed. Our own agent caught it. If we hadn't found out about it, we would have had a problem. The owner agreed in the contract to pay the second mortgage. We also had her replace the gas water heater, which was dilapidated and jerry-rigged to the gas and water mains, and looked like a disaster waiting to happen.

We recorded the contract at a title company. Anyone who does deals on the kitchen table without checking to ensure that the chain of title insurance has not been broken is looking for trouble. Just because you have the deed and you're the legal owner does not guarantee that you can sell the property. If you don't have title insurance, no bank in the country will finance the future sale of that house. Title companies won't insure the title if the chain is broken. It can take a minimum of months and as much as $15,000 to do a quiet title action to restore title integrity.

If a previous owner suddenly thinks they have a right to the property and sues the present owner, the title company will be liable. That is the protection you get with title insurance and explains why a bank will not finance a property without title insurance. Without title insurance, you may have $300,000 equity in a house, but when you go to sell it, no bank will finance the new owner. When you have five or six properties without title insurance, it's time to panic. In your mind, you have a million dollars in cash. And then poof, you don't.

This is an important part of investing right now, and something we teach in our classes. *The lack of title insurance can destroy a deal.* A lot of real estate investment advisors don't know that, because they spend more time advising than actually doing deals.

The more protections you buy—title insurance, home inspections, home insurance—the greater the odds that nothing untoward will happen to you. Don't skimp on sensible insurances.

Heatherwood rented very quickly. We were encouraged with

SUMMARY—Heatherwood

Source: Found through our buyer's real estate agent.

Formula: Bought subject to existing financing and sold as a lease-option.

Purchased for: $184,000.

Sold for: $223,000.

Collected: $5,000 option fee.

Profit on sale of house: $39,000.

---

our progress to buy 52 homes in 52 weeks. We felt we were on a roll with owner-carries—another term for buying subject to existing finance. The Las Vegas market was brimming with properties with little or no equity, and the market overall was sluggish in the winter of 2003. As a result, many people were motivated to sell with terms favorable to the buyer. Houses were very easy to pick up and easy to negotiate. It was one of the wildest times we had ever experienced. There were many properties described variously as owner-carry, owner will carry (OWC), take over payments, desperate seller, lease-option, make offer, or facing foreclosure.

However, under these same circumstances, it can be difficult to find good tenants, as they, too, can relatively easily buy a property. Interest rates had plummeted dramatically. Anyone with aspirations of purchasing a home was able to at least try to buy at that time. Even tenants felt it was as cheap to own as to rent. Finding tenants became an art form, one we describe later in the book.

HELPING A WIDOWER

There's a tragic background to Willow Pond Court. This house was owned by Mr. and Mrs. Faye, a retired couple. When Mrs. Faye died, Mr. Faye wanted to get out of the house. Emotionally he couldn't stay there. However, they had bought the house only four months earlier, and there was an early repayment penalty with the lender.

The house had cost around $200,000. The prepay penalty was $15,000, plus Faye would have had to pay a selling commission of 6 percent—about $12,000. If he sold the house on the market, he faced a loss of $27,000 plus closing costs.

Faye's other choice was to deed the house to us. We paid him $5,000. The difference to him was more than $30,000.

Our renter was a pool maintenance man who had bad credit after a divorce. We met him at an open house of ours, and liked him. He didn't like our open house but told us he would give us $5,000 as an option fee if we found a house he wanted. That house was Willow Pond Court.

Any time someone came to an open house and didn't like it, we asked them why. Was it the price? Was it the way the house looked? We talked them into telling us what they wanted. We told them we had homes all over the city and showed them flyers of different homes (we kept a stack in the car trunk). It suddenly dawned on us that finding tenants for existing houses might be a lot more difficult than finding houses for prospective tenants.

SUMMARY—Willow Pond Court

Source of house: Buyer's real estate agent.

Source of tenant: Prospective tenant who didn't want an existing house we had for lease.

Formula: Bought subject to existing finance and sold as a lease-option.

Purchased for: $200,000.

Sold for: $240,000.

Profit on sale of house: $40,000.

Again, we simple needed to ask for help—in this case, to ask anyone who looked at a property of ours but didn't rent or buy it, what it was they were really looking for. We started to shift our focus from finding tenants for our vacant homes (tough in the market at that time) to finding homes for potential tenants (easy at that time).

BUYER'S AGENTS

Most real estate agents represent sellers (which explains why the seller pays the commission on a successful sale). Not unexpectedly, these agents will try to sell you a property for which they have a listing. Buyer's agents on the other hand are professional real estate agents who specialize in representing buyers looking for real estate. For buyer's agents, any property on the market may be evaluated for the client.

Part of our strategy was to create a very clearly spelled out list of criteria as to what we were looking for. For instance as we have mentioned before, we wanted only 3/2 or 4/3 homes in particular ZIP codes, and no more than five years old. We managed to put all the information on a single page (see the Investment Strategy Worksheet on page 30), and faxed this page to the top 20 real estate agents in Vegas.

We received several calls inviting us to lunch and rides in luxury cars to look at listings. Gene told agents he had his own truck and didn't need a taxi driver to see real estate. However, he received an unending stream of e-mails from a real estate agent with lots of properties conforming to the criteria we specified. That agent was Katie Simmons.

Katie never called. She just kept e-mailing properties for us to consider. She didn't ask us to sign an exclusive (unlike other agents who said they could not work with us without an exclusive). Katie just sent us deals and made offers on our behalf. She brought us properties being prepared for foreclosure. She brought us homes where the owner would carry financing for three to five years. She introduced us to areas we were not familiar with. It was all great fun. She sent us hundreds of leads. Sometimes Gene sent out 20 to 30 offers in a two-day period, always 20 percent below asking price. Katie always submitted every offer we made.

Most of the offers weren't accepted, but some were. And we often received counteroffers that still fit within our criteria. "I'd come home and my fax machine would literally be stacked with counteroffers," Gene said. "I'd just sign and refax, sign and refax. I had no idea where some of these houses were. We bought places we'd never even seen. After we'd bought them, we would go there and say, 'These are great!' Once the buying machine gained momentum, and once we understood which of our ZIP codes were the hottest, we didn't care. We just said, 'We want that ZIP code. The house is only three years old. Just get it. I don't need to drive by it or see what the landscaping is like. Just get it!'"

We gave Katie fifteen $5,000 checks to use as earnest money deposits. We could have used less than $5,000, but with the crazy offers we made, we wanted to show we were serious. If you work with a buyer's agent, and they bring you a deal that fits your criteria, do the deal! If you walk away, the agent may never work with you again. Why would you not want to do it, anyway, if the deal fit your criteria? Buyer's agents are a great way to go. They have access to the MLS, bring you great deals, and make all offers.

We always put in our contracts "Subject To Final Inspection." That was our way out of the deal if the home was not in good condition.

There were no doubt times when Katie wanted to fire Gene. "I was very crazy and very stressed out," he said. "You can imagine the pressure of finding a home a week."

We also used the newspaper, flyers, and networking with business cards. The most calls Gene received were when we ran "STOP Foreclosure" ads in the Money to Loan section of the Sunday newspaper. We received 70 calls a month from that ad alone.

Katie was also very active in finding us owner-carry financing. Owner-carry financing is one of the safest ways to purchase. You take over equitable interest in the property, but the seller remains on the loan. It doesn't affect your ability to purchase more homes. The beauty of owner-carries is that you can acquire homes without needing to go to banks for financing.

The Advantages of Using a Buyer's Real Estate Agent

They have full access to the MLS—Multiple Listing Service.

They can send out hundreds of offers on your behalf.

They get paid by the sellers, so don't cost you a penny.

They write all the contracts—this is a great time saver.

If you are new and inexperienced, they are a wonderful team member to consult for information on anything from the market in general to a property in particular.

The moment your contract goes unconditional, they can use the MLS to attract a tenant-buyer for the home you do not even own yet.

They can run comps (comparable properties) for you.

Gene called Dolf and told him pre-foreclosures were becoming very time-consuming. He had to sit down with owners and go through a lot of hoops to extract the truth. There were four or five hours of negotiating and discussion, then another three or four hours of negotiating with bankers. Pre-foreclosure houses were also a bit more rundown than the owner-carry houses. If someone *has* to sell, the property is usually distressed. In owner-carry situations, there were still financial problems, but the owners usually just needed $5,000 to get out of town.

The main problem was that we had set ourselves a challenge: Buy 52 homes in 1 year. We needed to speed things up.

Gene called Dolf. "I suggest we pick up the pace here and start making offers on hundreds of homes through our buyer's agent," he said.

"Agreed!" said Dolf.

Once again, the importance of having good team members became apparent.

WHEN WE PARTY, WE LIKE TO PARTY

Some houses are haunted by tragedy. Orange Sun was possessed by party spirits. The house belonged to a disc jockey and a beautiful German flight attendant, a really nice couple. She was concerned about her job. It was post 9-11, and they weren't sure whether the airline would move her to another city. "His job was a little uncertain, too," says Gene.

The house was a nice three-bedroom, two-bathroom single-story home in Summerlin, within walking distance of the best private school in Vegas.

They couldn't sell the house because they had a huge prepayment penalty on it, and they didn't know what they were going to do. The other problem was that the mortgage interest rate was very high; it was a bad mortgage. There were also special assessments by the city. These are levies that the city charges to pay for new schools, parks, firehouses, and other infrastructure. The monthly total came to nearly $1,900. There was no way that we could get enough rent to cover that.

Our strategy was that because it was in such a highly-appreciating area, we were willing to take some cash flow losses for a while. Annual appreciation was well into the double digits. The strategy paid off. We bought the home for around $180,000. Within a year it was worth about $250,000. We ended up doing a two-year lease-option. The sellers moved to Florida, where they were doing well (we knew because they, like many of our other sellers and buyers, sent us Christmas cards thanking us for helping them).

We had a hard time renting the house, despite the fact it was only four months old. A young woman from California contacted us after a few weeks, wanting to rent it for $1,500 a month. We couldn't afford to let it sit vacant any longer. We were willing to go negative since it was a new home, and in Summerlin.

When that woman moved in, Orange Sun became a party palace. She flew in from Los Angeles with her friends once a month and used it as her Vegas party house. They caroused for a week at a time. The stereo boomed all night long. Neighbors found condoms tossed on their cars. Oddly enough, we never heard any complaints.

Then in a flash the tenant abandoned the property and disappeared. The house was trashed: holes in the walls and carpets ruined. Our attorney found her in California. She owed us two months' back rent and $5,000 in damages. When we reached her, she said, "My brother did it." We had a default judgment passed against her.

Now we had to find an attorney in California to serve her. We also had to change the judgment to $10,000. If we went for $5,000, the attorney would take $3,000 and we'd be left with $2,000. It all boiled down to the fact that it was going to cost us money to get our money. We didn't want to let her steal our $5,000.

A real estate agent selling one of the new high-rise condos

on the Strip did a rent-to-own for $5,000 down and a final payment of $329,000 in two years. Cash flow was still negative, but the home's value was increasing by 50 percent per year.

We had to cash out the original owner by early January. We started setting up financing in early October. Closing was scheduled for November, but when the time arrived, the lender didn't like the contract and wouldn't fund it 100 percent, as we'd hoped. We didn't want to put any more money into the deal. Gene thought he could find another lender to completely finance the house because there was so much equity in it.

Another attempt failed over the Christmas holidays. In the meantime, the flight attendant and the DJ divorced. The flight attendant, who owned the house, was in dire financial straits and afraid. She needed money desperately and was anxious to close.

By the first week of January Gene was increasingly agitated with his broker. Gene told the broker to close the deal, no matter what he had to bring in. By now Gene was worried we'd lose the house. If we didn't cash out the flight attendant by the time the contract expired, she'd get the home back.

In early 2005, hordes of people refinanced because of historic low interest rates. Mortgage brokers worked overtime for weeks. Gene's broker waited until the final day of the contract to put the financing in place.

The flight attendant sensed we wouldn't execute the contract and she'd get the home back. Her agent was also pushing her not to give us any extensions. She wanted to get the listing again and sell the house for a $200,000 profit. Gene didn't particularly like the thought of that happening. He also hadn't alerted Dolf to the impending disaster. There was also the tenant who had a lease-option contract. He could have sued Gene for not delivering the home.

As is usual when time is at a premium, the mortgage broker wanted five or six additional documents at the last moment before funding the deal. First, Gene had to prove he was moving out of his house into the Orange Sun house. Then he had to run to the bank to pick up updated statements to prove he had enough money to pay the mortgages.

Meanwhile, the escrow agent had a family crisis and needed to go home early. Gene was more than a little tense at this point. "I don't like using stern language, but I did," he admits. He sped to the bank, hurtling through traffic white-knuckled and sweating. A lot rode on the next few hours. He arrived at the bank, faxed the documents the lender required, then slipped $300 to the escrow agent to get her to stay.

His phone rang. It was the flight attendant's agent. The flight attendant refused to sign the contract. She wanted the home back. It was almost 5 P.M.

SUMMARY—Orange Sun

Source of house: Buyer's real estate agent.

Source of tenant: Open house.

Formula: Bought subject to existing financing and sold as a lease-option.

Purchased for: $225,000.

Sold for: $306,000.

Projected profit on sale of house: $81,000.

At that exact moment, the funding kicked in. The escrow agent told the flight attendant's agent the funding had begun. She added that by law we were in compliance with the contract, had fulfilled our obligation, and this would be the escrow company's position if the situation went to court.

Gene stopped shaking. The deal wouldn't be over until the flight attendant came in the next day to sign the papers. Luckily, she did. She went off the loan and walked away with $18,000, disappointed she missed out on a potential $200,000 profit.

The flight attendant saw only what she wanted. She didn't see what we had done for her. We had gotten her out of a bad spot when she had no other options. We had always made her payments, even when the property was vacant for three months. We had paid to fix all the damage from the L.A. partygoers.

The lease-option tenant can buy the house in just a few months. If he does, we will make about $81,000. If he doesn't buy the house, which is currently worth about $400,000, our profit will be closer to $175,000 based on today's values. Either outcome will be good. Property can be very lucrative, but it comes with some stress. All these events (some of which are still ongoing) relate to just this one property, and we had a lot more.

THE "LOOKS TOO GOOD TO BE TRUE, BUT IT WASN'T" DEAL

Two of our students hired Gene for personal instruction one weekend. They paid him to take them out in Las Vegas, drive around town, find a deal, and try to consummate it. Gene was a little leery. "I don't mind making my own mistakes, but . . . ," he said.

The man was a handsome, wealthy playboy. His partner fancied herself an interior decorator. She imagined redecorating every house we looked at. Real estate investment is about the market, not about hoping to add another $20,000 to the value of the house with black Italian marble. "It's sticks and bricks, guys. Don't get attached, and don't nest," Gene admonished.

We found South Fair Bluff that weekend. The back yard was small, but the house had fantastic unobstructed mountain views. It was owned by an investor, Mr. Garnett, who wanted to unload some of his underperforming assets. Sometimes you shake hands with people and immediately like them. At other times you shake hands with people and think, Where's my watch? Garnett was the latter type.

Gene first made sure Garnett owned the house. "A lot of times, believe it or not, people in Las Vegas will try to sell things they don't own." Gene looked up the home on the county assessor's web site, and found out Garnett did indeed own it.

The house was offered as a lease-option. Mr. Garnett was nonnegotiable on the monthly rental of $1,500, but the option exercise price seemed fair. Gene figured prices would rise some 13 percent (good appreciation in any market) and told our two students that at 13 percent over two years, they'd make a tidy profit. "We pulled up the records on a laptop, did our due diligence, and closed the deal with Garnett in a Starbucks."

As it turned out, property values went up by a massive 70 percent over the two years, and the profit they thought they would make was dwarfed by the actual profit.

When you think about it, a lot of people go to college and spend four years studying to get a degree at perhaps $25,000 per year. They outlay $100,000 to get a qualification that might get them a job at $40,000 a year.

On the other hand, Dolf and Gene were running courses in Las Vegas, where they charged fees that many people thought were outrageous: $4,000 for a classroom-style weekend event, and even $20,000 for a long weekend with six serious investors with no fixed agenda. They had one private student—a retired airline pilot—who paid $30,000 for a weekend of two-on-one instruction. Many people thought these rates were outrageous and spared no effort in letting us know their thoughts.

Yet the airline pilot made $140,000 within two months. Most of our students earned their course fees back within a month, and many earned it back tens and even hundreds of times over. Here's the question. Which is better: spending four years and $100,000 to figure out how to make $40,000 per year, or spending a weekend and $30,000 to figure out how to make $140,000 in two months?

Of course that's not to say everyone who spends $30,000 can make $140,000, but the whole point of what we did with the 52 houses in 52 weeks was to show that anyone can go out there and buy successful deal after successful deal. We now have a slew of students who are living proof this is indeed possible.

FEEDING FRENZY

Gene's niece, Cassie Siegler, had purchased a new home on a street called Munos in an area called The Vistas, one of the last pristine areas in Las Vegas. Up against Red Rock Canyon National Monument, it overlooks the entire valley. Gene felt that this was possibly the best area of all to invest in.

Cassie secured her position in another new property for

$2,000, with the home to be completed within eight months. Listening to her and the process she was going through was fascinating, especially the appreciation rates she was getting in that area. Gene immediately contacted our buyer's agent, Katie, and requested that she give him information on buying these particular spec homes. We still planned to continue buying pre-foreclosure homes, but all of a sudden the spec home market sounded very interesting. Katie found us Grotta Azura.

The Grotta Azura house was a turning point in our challenge. Most sellers were in some type of distress like divorces or fleeing Las Vegas for hometowns. It took a lot of time to look at distressed homes. When home owners fall behind in the payments, they disassociate themselves from the property. They stop watering and mowing the lawn. They ignore maintenance and take their discontent out on the property. We could drive down the street and immediately tell which homes were going into foreclosure.

Since part of our strategy was to put no more than $5,000 into each investment property, it became tough to find distressed properties meeting our criteria. Meanwhile, a new market sprang up all around us. Builders started constructing new homes in the ZIP codes we were investing in. They offered unbelievably low interest rates and no money down deals to get buyers into the properties.

Grotta Azura was this type of property. It was a second- or third-phase home on a corner cul-de-sac lot with a view of Red Rock Canyon Park and the city. The builder required only $2,000 down in earnest money. The property was to be finished in six months. At that time we'd bring in our own financing or go with the builder's financing and bring no

---

SUMMARY—Grotta Azura

Source of house: Buyer's real estate agent.

Source of tenant: Marketing on our Las Vegas web site.

Formula: Bought off the plan (closed with builder financing) and sold as a lease-option.

Secured for: $2,000.

Purchased for: $250,000.

Sold for: $495,000.

Projected profit on sale of house: $245,000.

---

money to closing. This was a dream come true: a $2,000 investment on a $250,000 home, which would appreciate before we had to bring in financing. Dolf was behind this 100 percent but was concerned Gene was going to have to sign for the properties under his name. Before that point we'd always required sellers to remain on loans until we sold the properties.

Gene was convinced he was onto a winner. The lot was close to one-eighth of an acre and had plenty of room for a pool that we arranged to have built and added to the loan. Then in the absurd market conditions of Las Vegas at the time, the deal got a lot better with a stroke of genius. As soon as Gene had contracted to buy the property, he started marketing it. He sent potential lease-option candidates in to view models the builder had onsite (to see what the home would look like) and to see where the lot was located. Before we had to close on the home, a lease-option tenant gave us a $5,000 option payment to secure their position in the property. We bought this 2-story, 4-bedroom home from KB Homes for $250,000 and resold it with a 3-year option for $495,000. It amounted to a built-in profit of $245,000 on a $2,000 investment (or *minus* $3,000 if you factor in the $5,000 option fee we collected from our buyer). Cash flow was neutral.

Since the market was not flooded with investors yet, Gene had plenty of time to invest in all the different builders' inventories. KB Homes wanted home owners to live on the property. Pulte Homes didn't care how many you bought, as long as you had $5,000 in earnest money.

THE BIG PICTURE

With our intense activity in the market, we started finding the path of least resistance. We learned to put in less money, with less risk, for higher returns. That is the name of the game! When you put no money into the deal, and keep someone else on the loan, then there is literally no risk. If a nuclear bomb goes off, you can say, "Look, I'm sorry, here's the deed back; good luck making the payments." There is simply no risk.

We had mastered the art of putting no money in (any earnest money or down payment we made was refunded through the lease-option fee we received from the tenant); we had someone else cover the rent (the lease-option tenant); we were not responsible for the loan (the seller stayed on the loan to the advantage of all parties; their credit could be restored this way); and, best of all, we legally owned the house. That is no-risk real estate investing. We are convinced this can be done anywhere in the United States and are delighted with reports from students of ours who have attended our events or purchased our course, *The Great Real Estate Investment Adventure*, that they are doing just that in many parts of the country.

Chapter 6

A SHIFT IN STRATEGIES

SURROUNDED BY INVESTORS

Crimson Rose was our first Pulte pre-build home. We were familiar with Pulte Homes because we owned some older Pulte homes and liked the builder. The house was a typical three-bedroom, two-bath and nicely built. Pulte had the best insulation system of all the builders we ran into, a special process that worked very well in the desert. The problem with Pulte was they sold mostly to investors. The entire tract had FOR SALE BY OWNER signs everywhere! To stand out from the crowd without putting much money in, we added a backyard spa. Pulte homes were harder to market because they all looked the same. We bought this house off the plan and sold it traditionally for a tidy profit.

We actually bought three of those. For $15,000 ($5,000 down payment on each), we were able to tie up three-quarters of a million dollars in The Vistas, which is most likely the best-appreciating area in Las Vegas.

Closing on the houses was staggered, so that we didn't have to finance all at the same time. The first one closed in August,

---

SUMMARY—Crimson Rose

Source of house: Direct from builder.

Source of buyer: Buyer's agent acting as listing agent for us.

Formula: Bought off the plan and sold traditionally.

Purchased for: $252,000.

Sold for: $322,000.

Profit on sale of house: $70,000.

---

the next in September, and the last in November. The difference between the Pulte homes we purchased and the KB home was that Pulte financing wasn't contingent on your using the house as your primary residence. KB had investor loans, but they required a $9,000 down payment. With $9,000 down plus closing costs, the deal became traditional. We weren't interested in traditional. However, we could do $2,000 for KB homes all the day long. We started looking for other builders who would let us secure property, to be built at a future date, with very little money down. Sometimes cracking the puzzle from a different angle was half the fun.

FINDING TENANTS IN DARK TIMES

By now the market was just starting to heat up. This was another scary time for us. Interest rates started to fall. Anyone who ever wanted to buy a home, even people with bad credit, could now do it. And we had 12 vacant homes. Twelve mortgage payments and other expenses such as property taxes, insurance and maintenance, without rental income to cover them, can be a problem. At an average of $1,200 to $1,500 per property, that amounts to $15,000 to $18,000 per month of cash-flow shortfall we'd have to compensate for. That's tough for anyone to sustain.

Dolf called Gene and said no more houses should be bought until they had figured out how to rent the ones they already had, as otherwise they were just acquiring negative monthly cash flow.

We decided we should develop systems, methods, and marketing techniques to find tenants. Gene wrote down every creative marketing idea he could think of or that he'd heard about or read about in books. Then, every day, he would go through his checklist of ideas to fill the properties.

The horrible truth is that when most people think of finding a tenant for their property, they have only one way of doing it. They go to a newspaper and place an advertisement in a Wednesday and/or weekend edition. There's nothing wrong with this, but it's also the way used by most other investors. They all place ads in the papers twice a week and sit by the phone hoping and praying someone will call and end up renting the property from them.

We started coming up with creative ideas. Some of them were very simple. One of the simplest methods was to put a sign on the front lawn so anyone driving by could see that house was for rent. You'd be surprised how many people driving down your street know someone who wants to rent, or even want to rent themselves. Don't just get a piece of cardboard and write on it with a Sharpie, in letters so large that you have trouble fitting the last digit. Get a professional sign from the likes of Home Depot. The cost is negligible. Put your number very clearly and simply so people don't have to get out of their cars to jot it down.

Another thing you can do is walk up and down the street to 10 or 20 doors in each direction. Knock on every door and say, "Hello, I'm the manager of 223 Oak Street. We're going to advertise it for rent, but before we do, if you have any friends or relatives moving into town, and you want them to live by you, please let me know." For every person who says, "You're really crazy, dude. Get out of here," you'll find someone who says, "Oh my God! That house is for rent? Oh my God! My sister is coming into town! I'd love them to live nearby! Let me call them! Oh my God! Don't rent it to anyone else!" You'd be surprised how often you can rent a property that way.

You can also print up a flyer with details of the property. Instead of going to 10 or 20 homes up and down the street, do it in a radius of two or three blocks so you might distribute 300 or 400 flyers. It sounds like a lot of effort, but, if after doing it, you get four calls on the property, and two callers say they want to rent it, you've got a tenant for your property and you have someone lined up for another property. The rewards for the effort are huge.

Those are three simple ways to find a tenant. There are many others we developed. We had houses by Nellis Air Force Base. We went up to the base and asked if we could put a notice on their notice board. They asked us what the notice would be for. We told them we specialized in renting houses to Air Force personnel, and that we had a house for rent.

Example of a Flyer Advertising a House for Rent

WANTED

Nice family to live in your Neighborhood!

We specialize in Rent to Own homes.
This means there are no banks to deal with
and you don't have to have perfect credit.

REWARD: $400

**For information leading to new home buyers
or to get a free listing of other rent to own
homes, simply call (800) 555-1212 or
e-mail** _____

**1234 Main Street
(800) 555-1212
www.website.com**

As Dolf relates, "At our events, we would often ask an audience, 'Do you really need to specialize in renting to Air Force personnel to make that claim?' Astonishingly, most people grinned and giggled and said, 'Of course not!' But the fact is, to stay within integrity, you do have to. And why would you not want to?"

Once, when the rent was not paid on time by a young officer, we made a phone call to the base. That same afternoon, a certified check was delivered with the comment that the base would sort the matter out with the officer directly. Who would not relish tenants like that? So yes, we absolutely do specialize in Air Force personnel tenants. And if you treat your tenants fairly, then word gets around and they will start referring other personnel to you.

In another part of town we had houses near a nursing home. We put a notice there saying we specialized in renting to nurses. Again, do we really specialize in renting to nurses? You'd better believe it. In yet another part of town, we have homes near a police station. We like having police officers as tenants. They tend to pay well, the neighbors love having a police car parked overnight occasionally, and are generous with referrals.

These are some of the creative ways we developed to find tenants for our properties. But the ultimate method, which we have already touched on briefly, was not to find a tenant for an existing property, but to find a property for a soon-to-be tenant. We were on such a roll, buying so many houses with such consistency, that we knew if someone wanted a two-bedroom, two-story home with a spa but no swimming pool, or whatever their criteria were, we could find it. We'd advertise for tenants and get potential tenants calling us. We'd say, "Look, we don't have anything right now, but we're in this game and renting all the time. Tell us what you want, and if we can get back to you in a week or two and show you some places, maybe you'd like to rent one of

114

---

10 Top Ways to Attract Tenants

10. Hold an Open House and place flyers everywhere.

9. Contact local religious centers and churches, and leave flyers.

8. Try getting a free link on the local Chamber of Commerce web site.

7. Post a professional sign on the property.

6. Have your buyer's real estate agent post the listing on the MLS.

5. Make business cards that have your Rent-to-Own information, and pass them out everywhere.

4. Run advertisements in local newspapers.

3. Knock on the neighboring 20 or so homes and let them know the house is for rent.

2. Distribute flyers for a two or three block radius.

1. Find the tenant first, and then find a house for them to rent.

---

them." We filled many properties because we found the tenant before the property. That was our ultimate method.

MOUNTAIN AND WALL VIEWS

A house on Mornings Dawn in northwest Las Vegas has an amazing view at the very rim of the mountains surrounding Red Rock Canyon. The challenge of the property was a very tall brown soundwall on one side of the property. An older investor had bought the house, but couldn't find a renter because of construction in the subdivision. He was a strange guy and an even stranger investor. Most investors put as little money into a deal as possible. He bought a new property that hadn't been built yet, and when it was finished, he paid cash. He liked to buy pre-constructed homes and sell them just as they were being completed.

He owned the house free and clear, and offered seller finance. We agreed on a specific interest rate, and the option for us to cash him out at any time by paying off the loan. We negotiated a monthly payment and a two-year owner note. He was convinced it was worth $230,000 and we were convinced it was worth $160,000. We met at $177,000.

When you have property that is not leveraged, you need to get your money out of the deal to do the next one. One thing Gene learned from Dolf was to always leverage investments. Real estate is the best leveraged investment on the planet. Remember our Grotta Azura home? With a $2,000 investment we made a $250,000 profit. We defy anyone to show where you can do that besides real estate, and still have the investment secured by bricks and mortar.

Cash-flow was negative by a couple of hundred dollars. Gene said to Dolf, "Look, I know it's negative, but the house is worth at least $200,000."

When we purchased the home, the gated community in which it was being built was not completed, with about 18 homes still being built. They were in the final phase. When all the homes were finished, a property identical to ours sold for $203,000.

We quickly ran into the same problems the previous owner had in finding a lease-option tenant. Nobody liked the

---

SUMMARY—Mornings Dawn

Source of house: Buyer's real estate agent.

Source of buyer: Buyer's agent acting as listing agent for us.

Formula: Bought with an owner-carry and sold traditionally.

Purchased for: $177,000.

Sold for: $260,000.

Profit on sale of house: $83,000.

---

soundwall. "I don't get what you don't like about it!" Gene protested.

Eventually we found a tenant, but he was always late with the rent. We had to keep sending five-day pay-or-quit notices. Finally, he moved out. A year later, we sold the home for $260,000. Oddly enough, the renter's daughter and boyfriend heard about other homes we had, ended up renting a different property from us, and turned out to be the best tenants we ever had.

A SUN-ROOM FOR A QUILTER

As soon as Gene's wife saw the Teetering Rock house, she wanted to move into it. It had a wonderful floor plan. It was a one-story property with a beautiful self-cleaning pool, way out in the northwest.

We purchased this from an investor who was offering an

owner-carry. It had a very interesting twist. We came in with $5,000 to secure the property, signed a deed of trust putting us on the title, and arranged an interest-only loan for two years at 7 percent. So, we were paying seven percent on the money with a balloon payment due in two years. The twist was that the seller was carrying a further two percent interest per month, which was to be included in the balloon payment. Effectively the interest rate was nine percent, with two percent accruing and being paid at the end.

We had a lot of people interested in renting the property. Many were trying to negotiate with us. Most just wanted to buy the property outright. We weren't interested in that, although we were offered a lot of money. We were interested in long-term buy and hold deals.

To fill the Teetering Rock house, we put an ad in the paper. An interior designer named Belinda who specializes in trade shows saw the ad and called for the address.

Belinda drove by and looked at the house. She was also a painter and quilter, and the sun-room caught her eye as a nice place to work on projects. She called her husband Rick, a tax consultant who represents people facing the Internal Revenue Service.

The couple had been renting for four years, ever since they had moved to Vegas from New Mexico, and wanted to buy a home. They had two sons, a 20-year-old enrolled at the art institute, and a 13-year-old. They'd done some house hunting but were discouraged by high down payments, "which we didn't have," Rick said.

Rick looked at the house. "It met my main criteria," he said. "It was single-story. It's a large open house. My wife liked it because it has a sun-room on the back." The whole family liked the pool.

SUMMARY—Teetering Rock

Source of house: Buyer's real estate agent.

Source of buyer: advertisement in newspaper.

Formula: bought with owner-carry financing and sold as a lease-option.

Purchased for: $249,000.

Sold for: $289,000.

Profit on sale of house: $40,000.

The family rented the house on a lease-option. "It was an easy experience," Rick said. "Everything was very simple." They are paying close to $1,700 a month, which is covering our mortgage.

The only concern Rick and Belinda had was whether the house would be worth the $289,000 they contracted to acquire it for. They need not have worried. The week they closed on the purchase, in May 2005, it appraised at $400,000.

SINGLE MOMSTER

Swan Brook was a beautiful two-story home in Summerlin with a Jacuzzi. The property overlooked the entire Strip. The owner was being transferred back to New York, couldn't sell it, and needed to get out immediately. We agreed on owner-carry

---

The Confidence to Buy Sight Unseen

At some point, you realize that you don't need to see every house you are considering buying before signing a contract.

Exactly when that occurs varies from investor to investor. But when you look at sufficient numbers of properties, you acquire a sense of the neighborhood and variations from house to house. In Las Vegas, which is very much a tract housing community (entire blocks are built with nearly identical homes), it gets easy to know what kind of house you are likely considering.

If you know the area and the price point, and you know that as long as the house is standing it has value, there is no need to drive by every home before writing a contract.

Bear in mind that we always had an inspector check out the home before going unconditional. If you are happy with the suburb, and the inspector is happy with the home, you can save yourself a lot of driving time.

---

financing. Swan Brook was another find by our buyer's agent, Katie Simmons. We hadn't even been in the house. We were so familiar with the area and the ZIP code that we started purchasing properties without ever seeing them. For Gene, this was the next shift in his investing education.

The house needed very little work and came with all of the appliances. We were a little surprised that the seller included in the contract that he was going to take the Jacuzzi. He ended up leaving it.

We found a single mother who worked for the county as a

SUMMARY—Swan Brook

Source of house: Buyer's real estate agent.

Source of buyer: From a sign on the property.

Formula: Bought as owner-carry financing, and sold as a lease-option.

Purchased for: $204,000.

Sold for: $264,000.

Profit on sale of house: $60,000.

---

corrections officer. She had recently been divorced and could not qualify for traditional financing. She had seen the home several times because her children had friends in the neighborhood. We had professional signs on all of our properties. When she finally called, we were able to get her into a nice, safe home in a great school district next to her children's friends. We had close to $60,000 in locked-in profits.

MODEL LEASE-BACKS

Up until this point in our quest to buy 52 homes, we had stuck to our plan: Buy three- or four-bedroom homes in highly-appreciating areas, in the $150,000 to $250,000 range. Then Katie Simmons contacted Gene and asked him if he was interested in taking a look at a lease-back property in north Las Vegas. He had never heard that term before so he went to take a look at it.

The house was a fully furnished model with all of the furniture, all of the upgrades, and all of the landscaping in place and included. It was a beautiful property. What the builder wanted us to do was purchase the property outright, and then he would lease it back from us to use as a show home for prospective buyers. Typically the rental income is 1 percent of the purchase price per month—a healthy return. However, the price the builder was asking was close to $300,000. We considered this too high for the area, based on comps, and so we opted out of that deal, but the concept was so fascinating that Gene immediately told Katie to start searching every builder in our target ZIP codes to find some model lease-backs. It didn't take long.

Silver Bark was our first model lease-back. It was part of the first phase of an upscale condominium complex. Usually builders sell the first phases of housing developments to pay for construction of the subsequent phases. First phases always include model homes.

A lot of people have still not heard of these. Silver Bark was a beautiful model on Town Center and West Sahara. It is vital as an investor to understand what is going on in the ZIP codes you are investing in. This area had been zoned for the largest upscale outdoor mall in Las Vegas and was going to be bordered by the next Station Casino, slated to be beautiful.

Since starting the 52-homes project, we had done a lot of marketing and networking in the Las Vegas area. Gene started to get calls from individuals interested in weekly corporate rentals. These rentals include bedding, linen, cable television, and other things that apartments are usually equipped with. These homes were perfect for corporate rentals. However, as

---

SUMMARY—Silver Bark

Source of house: Buyer's real estate agent.

Source of buyer: From our Las Vegas web site.

Formula: Bought as owner-carry financing, and sold as a lease-option.

Purchased for: $234,000.

Sold for: $370,000.

Projected profit on sale of house: $136,000.

---

with many model lease-backs, the numbers just didn't work for us, and we were unable to get the deals to work.

Nonetheless we liked the area, bought a piece of dirt, and with $7,000 down, had an identical home built for $234,000.

BACK TO HAWAII

The Capparro house was owned by a Hawaiian family who had had enough of Vegas. They had had the property on the market for several months. It fit our ZIP code requirements, and we made several low ball offers on it.

"I still today cannot believe I didn't jump on it sooner because it was a four-bedroom, three-bath in Summerlin in a gated community," Gene said. "In retrospect, there were so many more homes in better condition and newer that I was

123

not impressed with this one. When I look back on this years from now, it would be akin to not buying something in Malibu, California, or Scottsdale, Arizona, for $150,000 that would be worth $1.5 million in 10 years."

But back then we were looking at new properties and weren't so hot on buying five-year-old homes. Gene was convinced when Dolf told him it was in Summerlin and was gated. Gated communities give a little more security and are a great marketing feature for homes.

When we finally bought Capparro, the Hawaiian family was getting ready for foreclosure. We had to take the home in the condition it was in. It wasn't bad, but it needed cleaning.

We went through so many different market shifts within one year it was fascinating. Since we started the challenge of buying 52 homes in 52 weeks, we had been desperately looking for some type of bank or lender to give us financing to keep going. Although we were doing very, very well, we were also trying zero-down investment loans.

Once again, our buyer's agent, Katie, came through for us. Katie found an amazing mortgage banker named Roger.

"Roger was the first individual whom I had ever met who was not only a big investor himself, but also a mortgage banker who had his real estate broker's license. He understood exactly what Dolf and I needed to do and what we wanted to accomplish. He did some of the most creative financing we'd ever seen."

Now it was time for us to use our own financing. Interest rates were at a 40-year low. We all had excellent credit and they were able to cluster three loans at a time to purchase these homes.

The Capparro home was a beautiful two-story, three-bedroom, two-bath home in the suburb's highest-appreciating area. About this time the Internet really started to kick in for us.

We started using web sites with sophisticated search engines for anyone interested in rent-to-buy properties. We would specifically buy the names of people interested in rent-to-buy properties in Las Vegas who had about $4,000 to put down as option money and would have more than $1,200 a month for rent. The exciting thing at this point was that the loan we secured was an unbelievable 4.8 percent three-year interest-only, which put the mortgage payment at just around $1,000, exactly where we wanted all our investments to be.

We were able to find a tenant-buyer who wanted to rent for six months to determine if this was the home he wanted to purchase. We explained to him he would need a year's lease, but that we would allow him at the end of six months to buy if he wished. The rent was going to be $1,395 a month. If he

---

SUMMARY—Capparro

Source of house: Buyer's real estate agent.

Source of buyer: From our Las Vegas web site www.rent toownlv.com.

Formula: Bought with a traditional mortgage and sold as a lease-option.

Purchased for: $208,000.

Sold for: $290,000.

Profit on sale of house: $88,000.

---

bought, it would move into a $1,495 a month, with a $5,000 option fee.

The great thing is we were starting to secure tenants at about the time we were ready to close on homes. We hadn't even closed on Capparro when we had received $1,000 from our tenant. This caused a change in our strategy. The safest way to invest in real estate is to find a tenant with some money but bad credit who wants to buy a house. You would be surprised how many people are in that category.

Chapter 7

NETWORKING

When you talk openly with a wide range of people, you will be surprised at how many want to help you get a good deal. Never miss an opportunity to network.

GENE'S NIECE

As related in Chapter 5, Gene's niece had put us onto some good deals. She needed some extra money to buy upgrades for her own home, so we arranged to take a position in her Munos property and do a lease-option and equity split. This was a wonderful opportunity to help Gene's niece, plus secure a position in yet another property.

OUR LENDER

We were working with our lender Roger, getting ready to close on three properties. Roger had bought some land in

Hawaii to build his dream home. To pay for the new home, he was going to sell some of his investments. He had about six properties, most of which did not quite fit our investment strategies, since they were older homes in lower-appreciating areas. They all cash-flowed, though, and Roger had one that did fit our criteria. The existing tenants were a wonderful husband and wife working on fixing their credit, who planned to buy the home in two years. We purchased the property with tenants in place, and we had positive cash-flow. This is an example of an investor who was not in trouble, but just wanted to liquidate some properties so he was able to buy another.

It was a perfect win-win for all three parties.

OUR LENDER'S LOAN OFFICER

Our new friend and mortgage banker, Roger, introduced us to his loan officer, Irene. Taking advantage of the low interest rates, she was ready to buy a larger home. However, she needed to sell her primary residence to qualify for the new loan. We agreed to take over her property. It just goes to show that even at your lender's office, you can network and find people willing to bring you great real estate deals.

TAX LIEN HOMES

Our property manager tipped us off to the benefits of tax liens. Tax lien certificates are another great real estate investment. Every state has them. Las Vegas has quite a few. What happens is that for one reason or another a property owner can no longer afford (or chooses not to pay) property taxes. Local and federal governments don't look favorably on this type of reneging.

Property taxes always take precedence over mortgages, so government agencies—frequently county officials—advertise a date and list of properties where the outstanding property tax debt will be sold as a lien that takes priority over any mortgage.

The format of tax lien sales varies around the country. In some areas they are run like an auction, with people bidding on the note and its associated interest rate. In Las Vegas they are run like a lottery. This is how they work.

You usually show up at the county courthouse. There may be anything from a handful to hundreds of people present. As you go in, you show your ID and they give you a number. At a predetermined time they no longer allow anyone else to get a number.

A property is described, including how much is owed on it. A random number generator then chooses a number. The number is called out. If it is yours, you either say yes, you want to pay the backlog of taxes, or no, you don't want that one. If you say yes, you then have 24 hours to bring a cashier's check for whatever is owed, to the county courthouse.

With many mortgages, the bank operates an escrow account to pay for taxes and insurance. However, if you do not pay the bank to cover insurance and taxes, then it is your responsibility as a home owner to make those payments. The bank will have no idea if you're failing to make those payments until they hear from the county.

The reason we continue to go to these events in Nevada is

because, in this desert state, for whatever reason, quite a few people have gotten it into their heads that paying taxes is either bad or unconstitutional.

From the date you buy the tax lien, the owner has two years to pay you back plus interest. If the home owner doesn't pay off the tax lien plus interest, and there is no mortgage on the home, the federal government will deed you the property. If there is a mortgage on the property, the banks get the first opportunity to purchase it from you.

Owning a tax lien certificate is really a no-lose situation. At worst, the money you spent paying off the tax debt will be returned, along with an interest rate, which is typically one percent per month. That's at worst. This is what the original owners must pay you to have your stake in the property (which takes precedence over any mortgage) removed.

If the owners or mortgagees do not pay you back (plus interest), the government will deed you the property.

The first time we went to a tax lien sale, there were 25 homes for sale and exactly 100 registered buyers. "You could reasonably expect that on average, every fourth person would get a home," Dolf said. "So your chances of getting a home are 1 in 4, or 25 percent. Between the two of us, we had a 50 percent chance that one of us might end up with a home."

A number of sales went through, and then #78 came up— Gene's number. It was a $2,500 tax lien. Would he take it? Yes, he would. After a few more houses, #78 came up again.

Given that the chance of any one person getting a certificate was only 25 percent, and that Gene already had two, he had single-handedly beaten the odds by a *factor* of eight. "I thought, I should have stood in line in front of Gene, because then I would have had #78, instead of #79, and I'd have two certificates," Dolf said. But then #79 came up, and Dolf got one. Surprisingly, #79 came up again, and Dolf got a second. "It was starting to get embarrassing, as we had about seven or eight colleagues and students at the auction with us, and they must have been wondering if the process was rigged somehow," says Dolf. However, even the officials running the sale expressed consternation when #79 came up a third time, and this time for a substantial home—the tax lien debt was for more than $16,000.

"I didn't know what the house looked like," Dolf said. "To this day I haven't seen it. The point is, I said, 'Yes, I'll take it.'"

At the end of the day, between the two of us, there was a 50 percent chance of winning one house, and yet we had acquired 5 or 10 times the expected result. It was just phenomenal.

Of course we did not own the houses per se. We merely owned the tax lien certificate. The owners typically have two years to pay back the debt plus interest, which in some states is as high as 18 percent per annum. If the debt is not paid off, you get the house. Of course, if there is a mortgage on the house, then often the bank will pay off the tax lien so that they are in first position again.

The chances of getting the house are therefore greater if there is no mortgage on the property. Then again, if there is no mortgage, the owners usually have plenty of cash, and nonpayment of property taxes is more of an oversight than a result of shortage of funds.

Either way, the chances of actually acquiring a property by buying a tax lien certificate are very slim. In Las Vegas, it's happened three times in the past 2,000 tax lien sales. In other words, you have a 0.15 percent chance of getting the house for the price of your tax lien certificate.

"Those odds are pretty small, so I acquire tax lien certificates for the cash-flow," says Dolf. "One percent a month is pretty good. Some states have 18 percent per annum. But here is an interesting observation. . . .

"A 0.15 percent chance of actually winning the house is pretty small, but it is still greater than your chances of winning at a casino (where the odds are stacked in favor of the house, naturally, to pay for all the opulence). Hundreds of thousands of people go to Vegas every week to blow maybe $3,000 gambling, with an almost infinitesimally small chance of striking the jackpot, and they lose the $3,000 they put up and certainly don't get any interest on it.

"With tax lien certificates, whatever money you put up you get back, plus you get interest on it, plus there is a (small) chance of striking the jackpot.

"Put another way, when you buy a lottery ticket, you lose your investment unless you win. But if you put $3,000 into a tax lien certificate, you will get either the $3,000 back, plus interest, or, if you don't get the $3,000 back, you get the house, which might be worth a hundred times more. I cannot under-

---

Tax Lien Certificate Tips

Go down to your local county courthouse and find out if they hold tax lien sales or auctions.

Attend the next auction, even if only as an observer to start off with. Find out what interest rates are offered.

Network with others present at the auction; you never know where your next deal is coming from.

stand why casinos are filled with tens of thousands of people, whereas tax lien sales can barely get 100 people to show up. Just as well, though, I guess."

OUR ODDS SHIFT

Around May 2003, the market took a dramatic shift, and the value of our investments ballooned.

About that time we were enjoying picking and choosing whatever properties we liked, rarely even leaving home. Katie just e-mailed us properties that were either distressed, owner-carries, or must sells—all different types of motivated sellers. We made offers via fax while we drank coffee in our pajamas, usually $10,000, $15,000, or even $20,000 below what they were asking. We'd negotiate the price or terms and pick up the property. However, everything changed.

For one reason or another, our offers on homes in nice areas and in good condition, in the range from $150,000 to $250,000, were no longer countered. We determined these properties were indeed getting multiple offers and staying on the market less than before. The market shifted from a buyer's market, where we could negotiate price or terms, to a seller's market. When an owner determined they wanted to sell, they put it on the market and received not only multiple offers, but offers that were $10,000, $20,000, or even more *above* list price.

In May 2003, Gene received an eye-popping e-mail from a local real estate market analyst. For the first time the median price of new homes cracked the $200,000 barrier. The $201,960 median price was $10,000 more than in November 2002.

The number of resale homes was also at record levels. There were literally 4,000 sales that month, 500 more than the previous record set in October 2002. The median price of a resale home in Las Vegas reached a record $163,000. Homes were appreciating on average at one percent per month. When we had started investing in Las Vegas, the appreciation rate was close to seven percent a year. It had almost doubled.

Based on this new information, we decided to shift our strategy. We accelerated our purchase of spec homes.

While we were going after the spec homes, we found what we call smaller boutique builders. They build in between the big builders. They are not the KB or Pulte homes, home builders everyone is familiar with, but smaller boutique builders who build in nice areas, rarely more than 70 or 80 homes at a time.

PHASE ONES

We secured our next property for only $2,000 down. When the Sweden Street house was finished, it was a beautiful two-story home near Lone Mountain overlooking the Strip. Several of our students also secured three or four properties in this great area on the same day. The quality and craftsmanship of the boutique builder was so impressive that we secured a position in a phase one, which means the ground had not been broken yet in a new phase in a very highly-appreciating Summerlin area. All investors want to get in on the first phase of a development, because it's the cheapest it will ever be. Piles of dirt are everywhere, trees are spindly sticks, and developers offer great deals to get the first residents occupying homes.

We were able to secure Sweden Street for $2,000. We bought a phase one home from Nevada Housing and also secured the number one position in a model lease-back in the same subdivision. Nevada Housing was a smaller boutique builder and very easy to deal with. They had smaller subdivisions and were more personable than the big players like Pulte.

PRETTY VIEWS WITH BAD GOLFERS

While we were waiting for our advertising to kick in, a new Pulte phase called Silverstone Golf Course had opened in northwest Las Vegas. The more we learned about spec homes, the more we were interested in the power of phase one purchasing: being one of the first buyers to purchase a home in a new subdivision. We've always felt golf courses have high appreciation and demand. People love playing golf.

At the time we were looking at this subdivision there was talk of reducing the number of new golf courses in Vegas. The worst drought in recorded history had gripped the Southwest for eight years. When you reduce the availability of golf courses, you increase the price of golf course homes. It is simply supply and demand. Fewer new golf course homes make your existing golf course homes more valuable.

The things people love about golf course living are the views and the quiet. The downside is bad golfers hitting your home and breaking your windows. You need a home that has a very big back yard. The trend in the new home market is shrinking back yards and the neighbors getting closer.

"That was when I was happy we were almost finished buying," Gene said. "If I didn't like the size of the back yard and the closeness of the neighbors, then neither would my prospective

137

tenants. The new homes now in Vegas are so close I could not live in them."

We secured a Pulte home for $5,000 overlooking a fairway and facing the beautiful mountain and clubhouse. With two of our students, we ended up purchasing three homes at that golf course that day. Pulte planned more than 60 phases. Most Pulte developments were appreciating at about $4,000 to $6,000 per phase. Even if they went up $4,000 to $6,000 every other phase, we'd have more than doubled our money or created close to $200,000 in equity on that property because of the number of homes that are going to be built around that golf course.

We bought our golf course house for $260,000 (with a lot premium of $40,000 added on) and installed a $30,000 infinity pool. The house—which has spectacular mountain views—is currently leased (the tenants declined an offer to lease-option it with an exercise price of $595,000). However, they did pay six months' rent in advance. We could sell it today for a profit of $300,000, but we may never sell it.

Chapter 8

BEING FLEXIBLE

MARKET CHANGES

When we started our challenge, we had to be certain that we were able to rent the homes to cover our mortgage payments. The most frightening aspect was what would happen if the market turned on us. We could not afford the majority of our homes producing negative cash-flow. We made sure that if the worst happened, we could turn to the federal government and place Section Eight tenants in our properties. For the homes we had, the government would allow us $1,150 per month for a three-bedroom, two-bath home. This was our exit strategy if things went badly.

"I could not understand other investors who were playing the high-risk game of future appreciation on high-end homes," Gene said. Some investors would buy $600,000 unbuilt homes hoping they would double before the home was completed. I am not saying that some very fortunate people didn't get lucky doing this, but I know more investors who got stuck with homes. Furthermore, the banks changed their rules, forcing you to own the home for a minimum of six months after clos-ing before selling it."

Our strategy when we started was to look at homes for around $150,000. Right now, because of the massive increases in value that have occurred since then, you would be hard-pressed to get anything for $150,000, even condos.

SUCCESS

We began this project to prove anyone can do it. We embarked on a program starting January 1 to buy one house a week for an entire year with no more than $5,000 invested in any one prop-erty. By mid-September, we'd filled our quota. In other words, we were well ahead of schedule.

For a brief moment, we thought, Should we continue this pace for the rest of year? Instead of buying 52 homes, should we see just how many we could buy in a year? "However, hav-ing done the 52 homes, I was reminded of some of the reasons I'd gotten out of residential," Dolf said. "I hadn't done any resi-dential property other than homes I'd bought to live in for some 15 years. I was reminded of the downside: the phone calls you get in the middle of the night from people saying, 'My lavatory isn't flushing' or 'My tap is dripping' or some other seemingly minor thing. I decided no. The goal was 52 homes, as opposed to how many could we buy in a year. The fact we'd achieved it well within the allotted 52 weeks spoke volumes on our determination, systems, and perseverance."

Chapter 9

WHY LAS VEGAS WILL CONTINUE TO GROW

We started doing pre-foreclosures almost exclusively. Toward the end we were doing a lot of other kinds of transactions. We bought model homes. We bought spec homes. We bought lease options and owner-carries. We even attracted tenants, and then found houses to put them into. We bought tax lien certificates. We bought using a variety of techniques, partially because doing one transaction almost identically 52 times over is pretty boring. We did different types of deals to keep the interest level high, but also because the market was continually evolving. It got hotter and hotter as the year progressed. Even after our buying spree finished, it heated up some more.

In July 2004, the market peaked spectacularly. Since then, prices have come off the top. There are currently 12,500 homes for sale in Las Vegas. It has changed from being a seller's market to a buyer's market.

At its peak, long after we had finished buying, if you put a home on the market, you'd get 20 or 30 offers literally within three or four hours, for $10,000 or $20,000 or even $40,000 above asking price. People were going crazy buying real estate.

Now it's become a bit of a buyer's market. Twelve-and-a-half-thousand homes on the market is significant.

"Interestingly, the media's reaction to this is to foster the belief that the bubble has burst or is about to burst," Dolf says. "Even the talk on the street from amateur pundits is that the market has turned, it's the start of a massive decline, and, just like the Roman Empire falling into disarray, it's the first vestige of evidence we're heading into a societal decline. My personal belief is that nothing could be further from the truth."

For reasons that haven't changed, real estate values in Vegas must and will continue to rise, despite the current slight hiatus. They have to go up because land is limited in Las Vegas, unlike other cities such as Phoenix, Arizona, where you can still build for many miles in all directions.

Land values must and will go up in Vegas. Right now maybe there's a slight decline because it overshot too much. Maybe people just got too crazy. Who knows, maybe this project and some of the events we did contributed to that craziness because we were encouraging people to get into this market. We were doing so unabashedly and unashamedly. Everyone who got in on our say-so has done very well. We've got people who've made hundreds of thousands of dollars because they followed this advice. We know of 21 families whom we induced to move to Vegas to invest.

"It's my firm belief values will continue to rise in the due course of time," Dolf says. Evidence of this is other industries moving in. Vegas used to be known as a gambling town, then it was Sin City, then it became an amusement center for families. People even go there to look at the art. Steve Wynn in his Bellagio hotel alone has more than $300 million worth of art work hanging on the walls. There are people who visit Vegas just for the art.

There are other industries moving there. The Port of Long Beach, in California, has a customs-bonded area. It's the third-largest port in the world after Rotterdam and Singapore. They've run out of space, so they're going to rail the containers in to Vegas, still under customs bond, and do the clearing in Vegas. Containers will then be distributed across the country from there.

Call centers represent another industry growing rapidly in Vegas. And Wal-Mart has set up one of its three main nation-wide distribution centers in Vegas. Whereas four years ago there wasn't a single Wal-Mart in Las Vegas, today there are 17 up and running with 8 more planned. Wal-Mart spends a lot of money doing research on where to put new outlets. For them to commit 25 Wal-Marts to one city is evidence that the city will grow.

"I'm sure that in 50 years' time we will look back on current prices in Las Vegas and its present size, and we'll say it was just a town ready to boom," says Dolf. "I'm putting my money where my mouth is. I believe Vegas will continue to grow faster than the national average in terms of job growth, real estate capital appreciation, new residential construction, personal income, and many other economic indicators."

We know all these facts about Las Vegas because we studied the market hard and work in this market. But that is not to say that it is the only market in the United States that will continue to do very well. Phoenix, Arizona, Atlanta, Georgia, San Francisco, California, and dozens of other real estate hotbeds will also continue to do well. How much time do you want to spend finding the perfect investment location, before you actually go out and buy a piece of real estate?

"Whatever you do, whether you get fired up from this account of Las Vegas or not, do something," Dolf said. "The surest way to poverty in retirement is to watch TV and do nothing."

Chapter 10

YOU CAN DO IT, TOO

Gene's entire life had been about pursuing the American Dream: having a lot of money, being able to help his family, to have a big house, and to go on vacation whenever he wanted.

He was very good at publishing and climbed the corporate ladder quickly. However, even at the pinnacle of his career, when he was making $300,000 a year, he'd drive around looking at mansions and think, What are these guys doing to be able to afford a house like that? Gene thought, I've just got to work harder.

He pursued the corporate career, did very well, and paid a lot of taxes, but he never hit that million-dollar lifestyle he wanted. Then the dot-com he was running lost funding through market conditions, and he found himself on the street. Rather than following the herd and looking for another company with better fortunes, Gene decided it was time to take fate into his own hands, and choose a market sector that was strong and not in decline. It just seemed insane to keep on trying the same old things that were not working.

He realized he had to do something else. When he sold his

condo in the Bay Area and made a cool $350,000 in one transaction, he said, "I get it. This is what I need to be doing."

What Gene took away from our 52 homes in 52 weeks project was confidence and power.

"No one can ever take this away from me; no one can ever fire me from this," he said. "I never have to go into an office and say, "Please, Boss, don't fire me." I can look at any home, in any market, anywhere, and determine what the value is, and whether it's a seller's market or a buyer's market. Now when I drive and see a mansion or a house on the beach, I don't say, "Will I ever be able to have that?" Rather, I say, "Do I really want that?"

"I could lose everything I have tomorrow and go out and do this again. No one can take that knowledge and confidence away from me."

Whenever you accomplish a dream or achieve a goal, your perception also changes. Homes are no longer an anchor to Gene. "They're just a place to keep my stuff out of the rain," he says. "It's almost sad that I'm no longer emotionally tied to a property. I don't say, 'Oh, that's where the Christmas tree will be, and I'll mow the lawn and walk the kids to school.' It's no longer that Norman Rockwell vision. But on the other hand, I know I can have any home I want. That gives me tremendous confidence."

Gene has met many other people who have learned how to earn real estate riches and have made a lot of money.

"You don't need a lot of money to do this," he says. "Five thousand was the max we put into any one home. We bought many properties with very little money down. The experience has enabled me to teach the methods to many others around the world. A lot of my success is a mind-set. I was afraid three years ago to have more than one mortgage. We acquired half our properties by getting sellers to stay on the loan. The other half were acquired using our own credit. I used to worry when I owed the bank my one and only mortgage. Now I owe banks millions and sleep better than ever before. We made money on each and every one of the 52 homes. Those we still own are all generating positive cash-flow, even though we have refinanced many of them and pulled more money out."

Dolf agrees. "Even though real estate is a large part of my life, it is easy to forget what it feels like when you just start out buying property. It is easy to forget that feeling, when you are poised to sign the contract to acquire your first investment property, where the mortgage is larger than your net worth, and you know that if you cannot get a tenant you are in big trouble, of your heart pounding in your chest, sweat beads starting to form on your forehead, and your brain screaming out 'Don't sign!'"

But when all is said and done, doing nothing is a lot riskier than doing something. Dolf concedes that the greatest test of willpower is to refrain from saying "I told you so," but despite his predictions that the market in Las Vegas would surge, he, too, miscalculated, and the mistake cost hundreds of thousands of dollars, if not millions. Dolf and Gene agreed to sell some of their properties on a lease-option basis, as the option fee they collected (typically $6,000) would be nonrefundable and would help with their cash flow and stated intention of not putting more than $5,000 into any one deal. Statistically, around 98 percent of lease-options are not exercised nationwide, and the house reverts back to the lessor. However, in the heat of the market in Las Vegas during Dolf and Gene's 52 homes quest, prices moved ahead so much that if a tenant-buyer could no longer afford to make the monthly payments, they realized that rather than walk away and give the house back, they would be better off selling and pocketing the difference between their option exercise price and the by then much higher market value. Of the more than 30 lease-options they had, all went through to sale. This unexpected shift in the market meant that Dolf and Gene made perhaps $40,000 profit with a property, rather than the $180,000 that could have been realized.

"In stating this, we are not seeking sympathy—we did very well as is," they conclude. "But it does highlight the fact that it is better to make mistakes than to do nothing at all."

And if you agree that real estate is one of the best vehicles for creating wealth, then you can start to focus on doing some deals, too.

Go out and buy a house. Learn how to take massive action. Buy one house a year for 10 years, and become financially free.

*   *   *

Treat everyone fairly, remember to have fun, and take control of your financial destiny.

Successful investing,

Dolf and Gene

Appendixes

Appendix A

AUTHORIZATION TO RELEASE INFORMATION

AUTHORIZATION TO RELEASE INFORMATION

Date:_____

Via Facsimile No. _____

TO:

_____
(Name of Mortgage Holder)

_____
(Address)

_____
(City, State, Zip)

By this written notice, I (We) authorize you to release any and all information regarding loan number _____ to _____, [if entity: "and its officers and/or agents or assigns"]. This authorization shall remain in full force and effect until rescinded by me (us) in a subsequent written notice of such to you.

I (We) further authorize you to forward any documentation regarding the above referenced loan to _____ by mail, facsimile, hand delivery, or any other manner of transmission.

_____   _____
(Borrower)   (Social Security Number)

_____   _____
(Co-Borrower)   (Social Security Number)

157

Appendix B

GRANT, BARGAIN, AND SALE DEED

This security document conveys ownership in real property in Nevada.
Any deed is a legal document conveying title to a property.

APN:

WHEN RECORDED MAIL TO:

Name

Street Address

City, State, ZIP

GRANT, BARGAIN, and SALE DEED

FOR A VALUABLE CONSIDERATION, receipt of which is hereby acknowledged,

_____

*** Name of Grantor ***

hereby GRANT(S), BARGAIN(S), SELL(S), and CONVEY(S) to

_____

*** Name of Grantor ***

that property in _____ County, Nevada, described as:
See Exhibit "A" attached hereto and made a part hereof.

(Exhibit "A" shall contain the legal description of the property)
OR you can state the legal description in this area.

Dated: _____

_____   _____
(Signature)   (Signature)

STATE OF NEVADA   )
) SS.
COUNTY OF _____   )

On _____ before me, the undersigned,
a Notary Public in and for said State, personally appeared

_____

personally known to me (or proved to me on the basis of satisfactory
evidence) to be the person(s) whose name(s) is/are subscribed to the within
instrument and acknowledged to me that he/she/they executed the same in
his/her/their authorized capacity(ies), and that by his/her/their signature(s)
on the instrument the person(s), or the entity upon behalf of which the person(s)
acted, executed the instrument.

WITNESS my hand and official seal

Signature_____

Name _____

LIMITED POWER OF ATTORNEY

This document authorizes one person to act on another's behalf.
It can grant complete authority or be limited to certain acts and/or periods.
It allows you to act as if you owned the property and helps
you change over the water, power, HOA, and so on.

LIMITED POWER of ATTORNEY

Know All Men by These Presents: That _____

the undersigned (jointly and severally, if more than one) hereby make, constitute, and appoint

_____

my true and lawful Attorney for me and in my name, place, and stead and for my use and benefit,
LIMITED TO THE REAL PROPERTY HEREIN DESCRIBED AS FOLLOWS:

Lot_____ (__) in Block _____(__) , as shown by map thereof on file in Book_____of
Plats, page_____, in the Office of the County Recorder of Clark County, Nevada

APN_____

Commonly known as

_____

(a) To ask, demand, sue for, recover, collect and receive each and every sum of money, debt, account, legacy, bequest, interest, dividend, annuity and demand (which now is or hereafter shall become due, owing or payable) belonging to or claimed by me, and to use and take any lawful means for the recovery thereof by legal process or otherwise, and to execute and deliver a satisfaction or release thereof, together with the right and power to compromise or compound any claim or demand;

(b) To exercise any or all of the following powers as to real property, any interest therein and/or any building thereon: To contract for, purchase, receive and take possession thereof and of evidence to title thereto; to lease the same for any term or purpose, including leases for business, residence, and oil and/or mineral development; to sell, exchange, grant or convey the same with or without warranty; and to mortgage, transfer in trust, or otherwise encumber or hypothecate the same to secure payment of a negotiable or non-negotiable note or performance of any obligation or agreement;

(c) To exercise any or all of the following powers as to all kinds of personal property and goods, wares and merchandise, chooses in action and other property in possession or in action: To contract for, buy, sell, exchange, transfer and in any legal manner deal in and with the same: and to mortgage, transfer in trust, or otherwise encumber or hypothecate the same to secure payment of a negotiable or non-negotiable note or performance of any obligation or agreement;

(d) To borrow money and to execute and deliver negotiable or non-negotiable notes thereof with or without security, and to loan money and receive negotiable or non-negotiable notes thereof with such security as he shall deem proper;

162

(e) To create, amend, supplement and terminate any trust and to instruct and advise the trustee of any trust wherein I am or may be trustor or beneficiary; to represent and vote stock, exercise stock rights, accept and deal with any dividend, distribution or bonus, join in any corporate financing, reorganization, enforcement or foreclosure, singly or in conjunction with others of any corporate stock, bond, note, debenture or other security; to compound, compromise, adjust, settle and satisfy any obligation, secured or unsecured, owing by or to me and to give or accept any property and/or money whether or not equal to or less in value than the amount owing in payment, settlement or satisfaction thereof;

(f) To transact business of any kind or class and as my act and deed to sign, execute, acknowledge and deliver any deed, lease, assignment of lease, covenant, indenture, indemnity, agreement, mortgage, deed of trust, assignment of mortgage or of the beneficial interest under deed of trust, extension or renewal of any obligation, subordination or waiver of priority, hypothecation, bottomry, charter-party, bill of lading, bill of sale, bill, bond, note, whether negotiable or non-negotiable, receipt, evidence of debt, full or partial release or satisfaction of mortgage, judgment and other debt, request for partial or full reconveyance of deed of trust and such other instruments in writing of any kind or class as may be necessary or proper in the premises.

Giving and Granting unto my said Attorney full power and authority to do and perform all and every act and thing whatsoever requisite, necessary or appropriate to be done in and about the premises as fully to all intents and purposes as I might or could do if personally present, hereby ratifying all that my said Attorney shall lawfully do or cause to be done by virtue of these presents. The powers and authority hereby conferred upon my said Attorney shall be applicable to all real and personal property or interests therein now owned or hereafter acquired by me and wherever situate.

My said Attorney is empowered hereby to determine in his sole discretion the time when, purpose for and manner in which any power herein conferred upon him shall be exercised, and the conditions, provisions and covenants of any instrument or document which may be executed by him pursuant hereto; and in the acquisition or disposition of real or personal property, my said Attorney shall have exclusive power to fix the terms thereof for cash, credit and/or property, and if on credit with or without security.

The undersigned, if a married woman, hereby further authorizes and empowers my said Attorney, as my duly authorized agent, to join in my behalf, in the execution of any instrument by which any community real property or any interest therein, now owned or hereafter acquired by my spouse and myself, or either of us, to be sold, leased, encumbered, or conveyed.

When the context so requires, the masculine gender includes the feminine and/or neuter, and the singular number includes the plural.

(Continued)

Witness my hand this _____ day of _____ 2006.

Owner _____ Date _____

ESCROW NO.
ORDER NO.
RECORDERS INSTRUMENT NO.

WHEN RECORDED MAIL TO:

_____

_____

_____

STATE OF NEVADA   } SS.
COUNTY OF _____ }

On _____ before me, the
undersigned, a Notary Public in and for said
County and State, personally appeared

_____
known to me to be the person ___ described in
and who executed the foregoing instrument,
who acknowledged to me that ___ he ___ executed
the same freely and voluntarily and for the uses
and purposes therein mentioned.

WITNESS my hand and official seal.

_____
Notary Public in and for Said County and State

Appendix D

BINDING LEGAL AGREEMENT

This document is used at the first meeting with a "motivated seller." It states that you and the seller will perform agreed-upon activities and enables you to have some written agreement while you do your due diligence. It is not completely binding, but it does offer some peace of mind by showing that the seller has agreed in principle to your offer.

BINDING LEGAL AGREEMENT

_____ ("Seller")

and

_____ ("Buyer")

Seller agrees to sell _____ (the "Property") for $_____.

Seller agrees to sell the Property for Buyer's simply taking over the payments of $_____ per month.

Seller agrees to allow access to all banking information regarding the Property.

Seller warrants that there are no other encumbrances on the Property.

Seller warrants that all taxes are paid and current, that the loan has not been recast, and that no forbearance agreement has been given.

Seller agrees to stay on the loan for at least _____ years.

Seller agrees to leave all appliances, fixtures, blinds, and so on in working order.

Seller is entering into this agreement willingly and warrants that s/he was not forced or coerced into this agreement.

Buyer agrees to cover payments associated with the Property.

_____   _____
SELLER   DATE

_____   _____
BUYER   DATE

52 Homes—
Some Photos

Emerald Waters—The first of our 52 homes.

Orange Sun—Bought from a disc jockey and a flight attendant; leased to a party animal.

Milbank Avenue—Sandwich lease-option bought from a bachelor
and sold to a couple with bad credit.

Silver Bark—Our first model lease-back.

Sweden Street—Brand-new property secured for only $2,000.

Crimson Rose—Bought off the plan and sold traditionally.

Grotta Azura—Bought with $2,000 down and builder financing, and sold as a lease-option.

Teetering Rock—Bought with an owner-carry loan, and sold as a lease-option.

Fairwind Acres—Another house bought with no net money going in.

One of two houses we bought on Wolf Dancer.

Dolf outside the Orange Sun home with our advertising materials.

Gene inside the Orange Sun home with brochures of other homes available.

White Quail—The Trans Am goes with the house!

Willow Pond—Helping a widower.

Mandy Scarlett—Another lease-option sale.

One of several tax lien certificate investments.

Mornings Dawn—This property led us to our best tenants.

Another house on Sweden Street.

Winter Thor Court—Sandwich lease-option.

Heatherwood—Hidden second mortgage of $20,000.

Rocky Bluff—Saved by a land trust!

Tahiti Isle—Never believe what you are told!

Blue View—The beautiful girl and the private eye.

Further Tips, Tools, and Information

Are you interested in seeing color photos of some of the 52 homes that Dolf and Gene bought? You can check them out at www.dolfderoos.com.

Dolf and Gene have run weekend courses in Las Vegas on how to buy real estate. These have been professionally recorded to create *The Great Real Estate Investment Adventure Course.* The course includes 10 CDs, a CD-ROM, and a 100-page workbook including all the documents you need, to do what they did. For more details, check out www.dolfderoos.com.

Are you interested in finding out more about the analysis software REAP? For screen shots, tutorials, FAQs, and download information, check out www.dolfderoos.com.

To be kept up-to-date with new product updates, events, and new products, please subscribe to our free newsletter at www.dolfderoos.com.

About the Authors

Dr. Dolf de Roos began investing in real estate as an undergraduate student. Despite going on to earn a Ph.D. in electrical and electronic engineering from the University of Canterbury, Dolf increasingly focused on his flair for real estate investing, which has enabled him to have never had a job. He has, however, invested in many classes of real estate (residential, commercial, industrial, hospitality, and specialist) all over the world.

Today he is the chairman of the public company Property Ventures Limited, an innovative real estate investment company whose stated mission is to massively increase stockholders' worth. Over the years, Dolf was cajoled into sharing his investment strategies, and he has run seminars on the Psychology of Creating Wealth and on Real Estate Investing throughout North America, Australia, New Zealand, Asia, the Middle East, and Europe since the 1980s.

Beyond sharing his investment philosophy and strategies with tens of thousands of investors (beginners as well as seasoned experts), Dolf has also trained real estate agents, written and published numerous bestselling books on property, and introduced computer software designed to analyze and manage properties quickly and efficiently. He often speaks at investors' conferences, real estate agents' conventions, and his own international seminars, and regularly takes part in radio shows and television debates. Born in New Zealand, raised in Australia, New Zealand, and Europe, Dolf, with six languages up his sleeve, offers a truly global perspective on the surprisingly lucrative wealth-building opportunities of real estate.

Today, Dolf is a Visiting Professor of Real Estate at the University of North Texas, and teaches at events and institutions in over 16 countries, including Tony Robbins' Wealth Mastery and Trump University. He appears regularly on TV networks including CNNfn, NY1, Fox TV, and ABC, and is heard on countless radio stations including NPR and Bloomberg Radio. His weekly video mentoring program is seen in 39 countries.

To find out what you can learn from Dolf's willingness to share his knowledge about creating wealth through real estate, and to receive his free monthly newsletter, please visit his Web site at www.dolfderoos.com.

 **Gene Burns** spent 20 years traveling the United States to launch high-tech magazines. However, with the dot-com boom coming to an end, Gene decided life in the corporate world was no longer for him and he was ready for a change. After his condo doubled in value in the San Francisco Bay area, Gene saw real estate as a way to leverage assets and achieve his goal of becoming financially free. Gene went into real estate full time. Within his first six months he completed 12 deals, and he never looked back.

Gene met Dolf at a seminar Dolf put on in San Diego. They realized they had several things in common: They loved life, they loved laughing, and they loved real estate. The two began working together. Shortly thereafter, they challenged themselves to buy 52 homes in 52 weeks in the Las Vegas market.

Today, Dolf and Gene continue to partner on new real estate projects.

Other Books by
Dolf de Roos

Real Estate Riches

An all-time bestseller, Dolf's classic *Real Estate Riches* shows readers from all walks of life how to find great deals and make great profits in the real estate market. This compelling book reveals why real estate is such a reliable moneymaker, and how novice investors and old pros alike can achieve the biggest return on their investment.

Full of time-honored wisdom, proven tactics, and quick-and-easy tips, *Real Estate Riches* will show you how to find the best properties, analyze deals, negotiate and submit offers, effectively manage properties, and dramatically increase the value of your real estate without spending much money. Dolf shows you:

- Why real estate is the best investment in the world
- How you can consistently find great deals
- The eight golden rules of real estate investing
- How to use tax laws to subsidize your investments
- How to create income using OPM (other people's money)
- The pros and cons of residential versus commercial real estate

Real Estate Riches has been on major bestseller lists in five countries, including those of the *New York Times, Wall Street Journal, BusinessWeek,* and Amazon.com.

With a Foreword by Alex Rodriguez and with over 500,000 copies sold, *Real Estate Riches* has taken on an almost cultlike status among both beginners and seasoned investors.

The Insider's Guide to Making Money in Real Estate

by Dolf de Roos and Diane Kennedy

The Insider's Guide to Making Money in Real Estate explains why real estate is a consistently profitable moneymaker and how everyday people can build their fortunes regardless of their credit score or how much money they have in the bank. It's true—you don't have to be rich to invest in real estate. It's the easiest, most leveraged method for building sustainable wealth over time, and it's open to everyone.

In this practical, nuts-and-bolts guide, *New York Times* bestselling authors Dolf de Roos and Diane Kennedy cover the basics of investing, and offer the kind of insider advice and little-known tips you won't find anywhere else. You'll get a wealth of bright ideas and smart investment moves, as well as examples, case studies, and true investing stories from successful investors just like you. You'll learn:

- How to spot great bargains in neighborhoods with great potential.
- How to finance your investments with less-than-perfect credit.
- How to find reliable tenants who'll pay top dollar.
- Everything you need to know about property taxes and deductions.
- How to use tax benefits to increase your profits.

The Insider's Guide to Real Estate Investing Loopholes

by Diane Kennedy and Dolf de Roos

The Insider's Guide to Real Estate Investing Loopholes reveals the best and most effective tax loopholes that successful real estate investors use to maximize their profits. This revised edition covers the new tax laws, and features new and updated case studies and examples.

Real estate is probably the best investment money can buy, in part because there are so many profit-maximizing tax loopholes that directly benefit real estate investors. In this practical and straightforward real estate classic, the authors show investors how to increase their investment profits and use real estate as a legal tax shelter. You'll find practical guidance on:

- Tax loopholes that turn your home into a profit center.
- Tricks for using your vacation home as a tax-saving investment.
- Real estate investment strategies for taking advantage of international tax laws.
- Creative cash flow techniques for increasing your investments' profitability.
- How to cut taxes through the 1031 tax-free exchange, pension funds, real estate loss deductions, homestead exemptions, and joint tenancies.
- Real estate pitfalls and how to avoid them.

101 Ways to Massively Increase the Value of Your Real Estate Without Spending Much Money

Not only does Dolf contend that there are 101 ways to massively increase the value of a property without spending much money on it, but true to form he sits down and details them in writing.

In this book, Dolf shares some obvious and some esoteric ways that you can easily increase the value of your property by far more than the cost of the improvement. If by spending $1,000 to build a carport, you increase the rental income of that property by $1,000 per year (which is a 100 percent return on your $1,000 investment), why would you not do it? Especially if, as Dolf shows you, you do not even have to come up with the $1,000 out of your own pocket in the first place.

You may not choose to implement all of the 101 ideas detailed in this book on one property, but there will be ideas here that you would never think of in a month of Sundays on your own. Why would you not implement at least some of them?

Extraordinary Profits from Ordinary Properties
For years, Dolf shared his experiences in the real estate market with people through his writings, his books, and his seminars. His success stories were so regular that people began to think that while it may be easy for *him*, it was not possible for *them* to achieve anywhere near the same sorts of results. Consequently, Dolf invited people on his database to submit photos and a brief description of properties they had bought, thinking that the submissions would lead to some interesting statistical analyses.

However, the stories that people submitted were so amazing, so enthralling, and so inspirational that Dolf essentially reproduced them verbatim to show how even ordinary properties can lead to extraordinary profits.

Originally written using examples from New Zealand, further editions are being compiled showing examples from other regions as well. Check out his Web site at www.dolfderoos.com for details on the latest editions.

Index

Page numbers in *italics* refer to photographs.

A

Addictions, motivated sellers and, 41–42
Adjustable-rate mortgages (ARMs), motivated sellers and, 39–41
Advertising, to find motivated sellers, 27, 31, 33–34, 35, 93
Analysis of potential deal, with REAP, 42–45
Anchor Drive deal, 76–79
Appreciation, *see* Capital appreciation
Authorization to Release Loan Information, 73, 85
sample form, 157

B

Bankruptcy, Chapter 7, 71–72
Binding legal agreement, 73
sample form, 166
Blue View deal, 83–84, *182*
Brown, Dan, 61–63
Business cards, for finding motivated sellers, 32–33
Buyer's agent, 91–94. *See also* Simmons, Katie

C

Capital appreciation:
in Las Vegas, 19
primary contributors to, 21–22
working in areas of highest, 27

Capparro deal, 123–126
Caruso, Monica, 18
Chapter 7 bankruptcy, 71–72
Climate, as factor in capital appreciation, 21–22
Crimson Rose deal, 109–110, *172*

D

Deal examples:
owner-carry financing, deed of trust, 63–67
owner-carry financing, land trust, 68–72
owner-carry financing, lease-option, 72, 74–76, 83–91, 95–99, 117–123
owner-carry financing, *lis pendens*, 76–79
owner-carry financing, traditional sale, 115–117
sandwich lease option, 56–63
spec homes, 101–104, 109–110, 136–138
traditional mortgage, lease-option, 123–126

Deed:
always having with you, 73
sample Grant, Bargain, and Sale Deed, 160
Deed of trust, Dusty View deal, 63–67
Divorce, motivated sellers and, 38–39
Dusty View deal, 63–67

E

Emerald Waters deal, 56–60, *178*
Employment outlook, for investment area, 21–22
Eviction, of tenants, 64–65
Existing financing, *see* Owner-carry financing

F

Fairwind Acres deal, *174*
52 houses in a year idea, *see also* Deal examples
Las Vegas as place for, 15–21
origin of, 8–9

stories and experiences
of doing, 13–15
strategy and, 25–52
Financial overextension,
motivated sellers and,
36–42
Finder's fee, 33
Flyers:
to find motivated sellers,
31, 33–34, 55
to find tenants, 112,
113

G

Gated communities, 124
Golf course homes, 137–138
Grant, Bargain, and Sale
Deed, sample form,
160
Grotta Azura deal, 101–104,
173

H

Heatherwood deal, 87–90,
180
Hidden second mortgage,
87–88
Holiwell, Larry, 74–76

I

Internet use, 124–125

K

KB homes, 101–104, 110

L

Land trust:
advantages of, 69
Anchor Drive deal, 76–79
checklist for buying with,
70
Rocky Bluff deal, 68–72,
181
LaRue, Eddie, 69, 71, 83
Las Vegas, Nevada:
population growth in,
15–21
real estate market in, 4,
15–21, 145–147
transient nature of
population in, 45–46
Lease-backs, 121–123
Lease-option:
advantages and
disadvantages of, 46, 68
Capparro deal, 123–126

Lease-option *(Continued)*
  Emerald Waters deal,
    56–60, *178*
  Milbank Avenue deal,
    60–63, *170*
Lease-option, owner-carry
  financing with:
  Blue View deal, 83–84,
    182
  Heatherwood deal, 87–90,
    180
  Orange Sun deal, 95–99,
    170
  Silver Bark deal, 121–123,
    171
  Swan Brook deal,
    119–121
  Tahiti Isle deal, 85–87,
    181
  Teetering Rock deal,
    117–119, *174*
  White Quail deal, 72,
    74–76, *176*
  Willow Pond Court deal,
    90–91, *177*
LIBOR (London interbank
  offered rate), 40
Limited Power of Attorney,
  73
  sample form, 162–164
Lis pendens, 76–79

M

Marketing strategy, *see*
  Advertising
Milbank Avenue deal,
  60–63, *170*
Mornings Dawn deal,
  115–117, *179*
Motivated sellers, 34–42
  finances and, 34–38
  learning to approach,
    50–52
  main reasons for
    desperation of, 38–42
  questions to ask of, 51

N

Neighborhood, learning
  about, 64–65. *See also*
  Capital appreciation
Neighbors, speaking with,
  55
Networking, with family and
  business associates,
  129–130
Nevada Housing, 137
Notary, 69, 71
Notice of Default (NOD),
  35

O

Orange Sun deal, 95–99, *170,
175, 176*
Owner-carry financing, 89
advantages of, 93
Mornings Dawn deal,
115–117, *179*
Owner-carry financing with
deed of trust, Dusty
View deal, 63–67
Owner-carry financing with
land trust, Rocky Bluff
deal, 68–72, *181*
Owner-carry financing with
lease-option:
Blue View deal, 83–84,
182
Heatherwood deal,
87–90, *180*
Orange Sun deal, 95–99,
170, 175, 176
Silver Bark deal, 121–123,
171
Swan Brook deal, 119–121
Tahiti Isle deal, 85–87,
181
Teetering Rock deal,
117–119, *174*
White Quail deal, 72,
74–76, *176*

Willow Pond Court deal,
90–91, *177*
Owner-carry financing
with *lis pendens*, Anchor
Drive deal, 76–79

P

Phoenix, Arizona, 4
Planning, *see* Strategy for
investing
Population growth:
in Las Vegas, 15–21
as primary factor for
capital appreciation,
21–22
Posters, to find motivated
sellers, 33
Pre-foreclosure seminars,
55–56
Private investigator, 83
Property taxes, *see* Tax lien
certificate homes
Pulte Homes, 104, 109–110

Q

Quiet title action, 78
Quitclaim, 39, 66

R

Real Estate Acquisition
   Program (REAP),
   42–45
Real estate agent, *see*
   Buyer's agent
Real estate investing,
   see also Strategy for
   investing
   courses in, 99–101, 105
   future of, 151–153
   hot markets for, 4, 15–21,
   147
Rental properties, *see*
   Lease-option;
   Tenants
Rocky Bluff deal, 68–72,
   181

S

Second mortgage, hidden,
   87–88
Section Eight tenants,
   141
Sellers, *see* Motivated
   sellers
Siegler, Cassie, 101–102
Sight-unseen deals, 120

Silver Bark deal, 121–123,
   171
Silverstone Golf Course deal,
   137–138
Simmons, Katie, 92–93, 120,
   121–122, 124
Smith, Dennis, 18
Spec houses:
   Crimson Rose deal,
      109–110, *172*
   golf course homes,
      137–138
   Grotta Azura deal,
      101–104, *173*
   Mornings Dawn deal,
      109–110, *179*
   phase one purchasing
      of, 136–138
   Sweden Street deals,
      136–137, *172*, *179*
"Stop foreclosure"
   advertisements, 93
Strategy for investing, 25–52
   house choice decisions,
      25–27
   marketing plan, 27, 31–34,
      35
   motivated sellers and,
      34–42, 50–52
   outline of and worksheet
      for, 28–30

REAP and, 42–45
willingness to take action
  and commit to plan,
  46–49
Summerlin, Nevada, 16–17,
  60–63, 123–124
Swan Brook deal, 119–121
Sweden Street deals,
  136–137, *172, 179*

T

Tahiti Isle deal, 85–87, *181*
Tax lien certificate homes,
  130–135, *169*
Teetering Rock deal,
  117–119, *174*
Tenants:
  creative ways to find,
    110–115
  default and, 56–60
  eviction of, 64–65
  federal Section Eight,
    141
  finding homes for, 90–91

with some money but bad
  credit, 126
Title action, quiet, 78
Title agent, 85–87
Title insurance, 88
Traditional mortgage with
  lease-option deal,
  123–126

W

White Quail deal, 72, 74–76,
  176
Willow Pond Court deal,
  90–91, *177*
Winter Thor Court deal, *180*
Wolf Dancer deals, *175*

Z

ZIP code, capital
  appreciation research
  and, 27, 28. *See also*
  Neighborhood

More from
Best-Selling author
Dolf de Roos

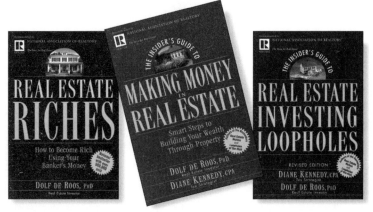